William Willis

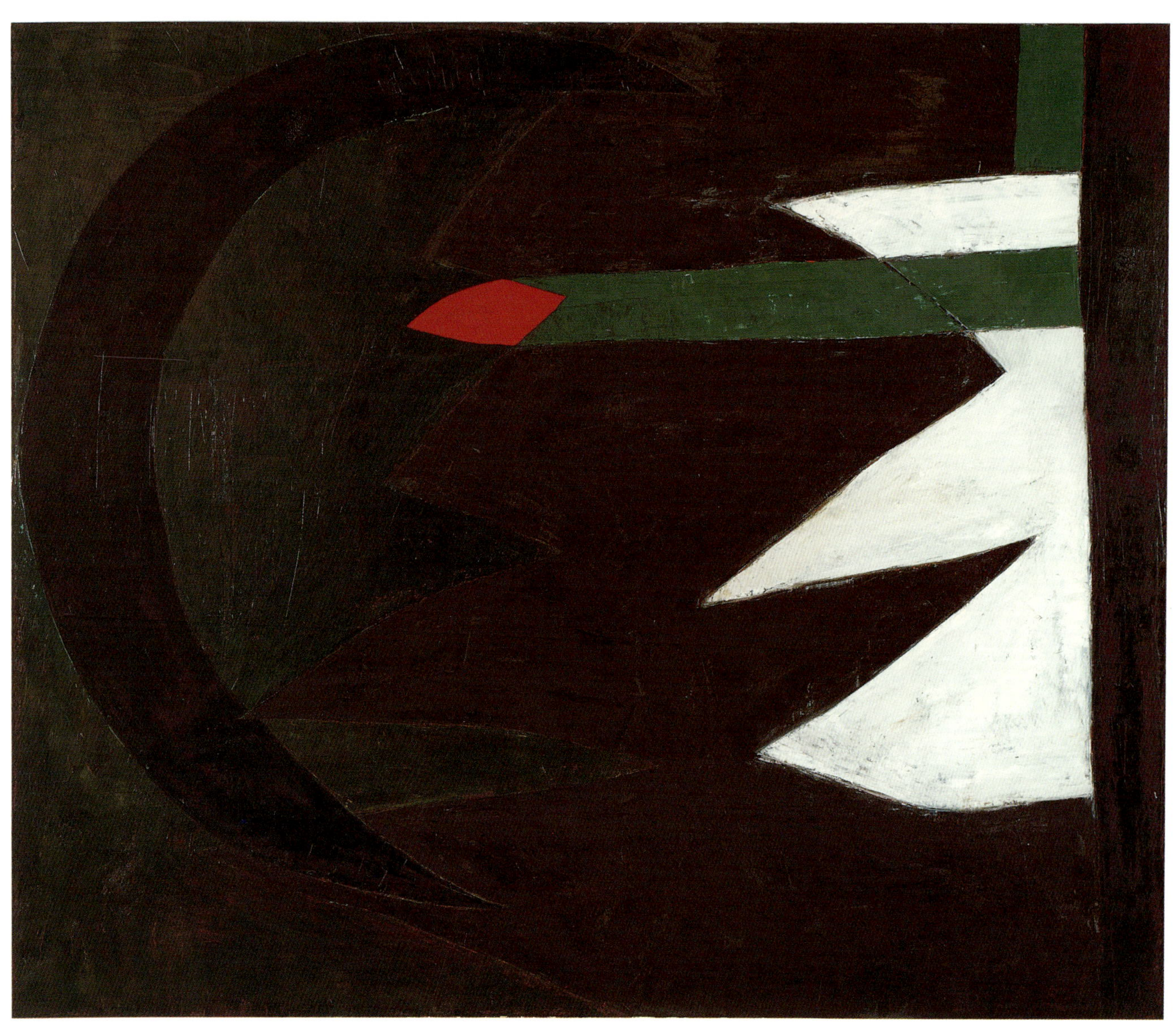

Cat. 4. *The Persistent Fool,* 1981, oil on canvas, 90 x 108. Courtesy of Baumgartner Galleries, Washington, D.C., and Rosa Esman Gallery, New York

William Willis

Contemporary Painting

LINDA L. JOHNSON

The Phillips Collection, Washington, D.C.
1989

This publication was prepared in conjunction with the exhibition, *Contemporary Painting: William Willis*, organized by The Phillips Collection.

Published by The Phillips Collection, Washington, D.C.

Library of Congress Cataloging-in-Publication Data
Johnson, Linda, L., 1961-
Contemporary painting : William Willis.
Includes bibliographical references.
1. Willis, William, 1943- --Exhibitions.
I. Willis, William, 1943- II. Phillips Collection. III. Title.
ND237.W725A4 1989 759.13 89-22854
ISBN 0-943044-13-8

Designed by Susan Lehmann, Washington, D.C.
Edited by Ellen Cochran Hirzy
Typesetting by VIP Systems, Inc., Alexandria, Virginia
Printed by Garamond/Pridemark, Inc., Baltimore, Maryland

Photography Credits: Edward Owen, cat. 4, 5, 7, 8, 9.
Mark Gulezian/QuickSilver, all remaining.

Contents

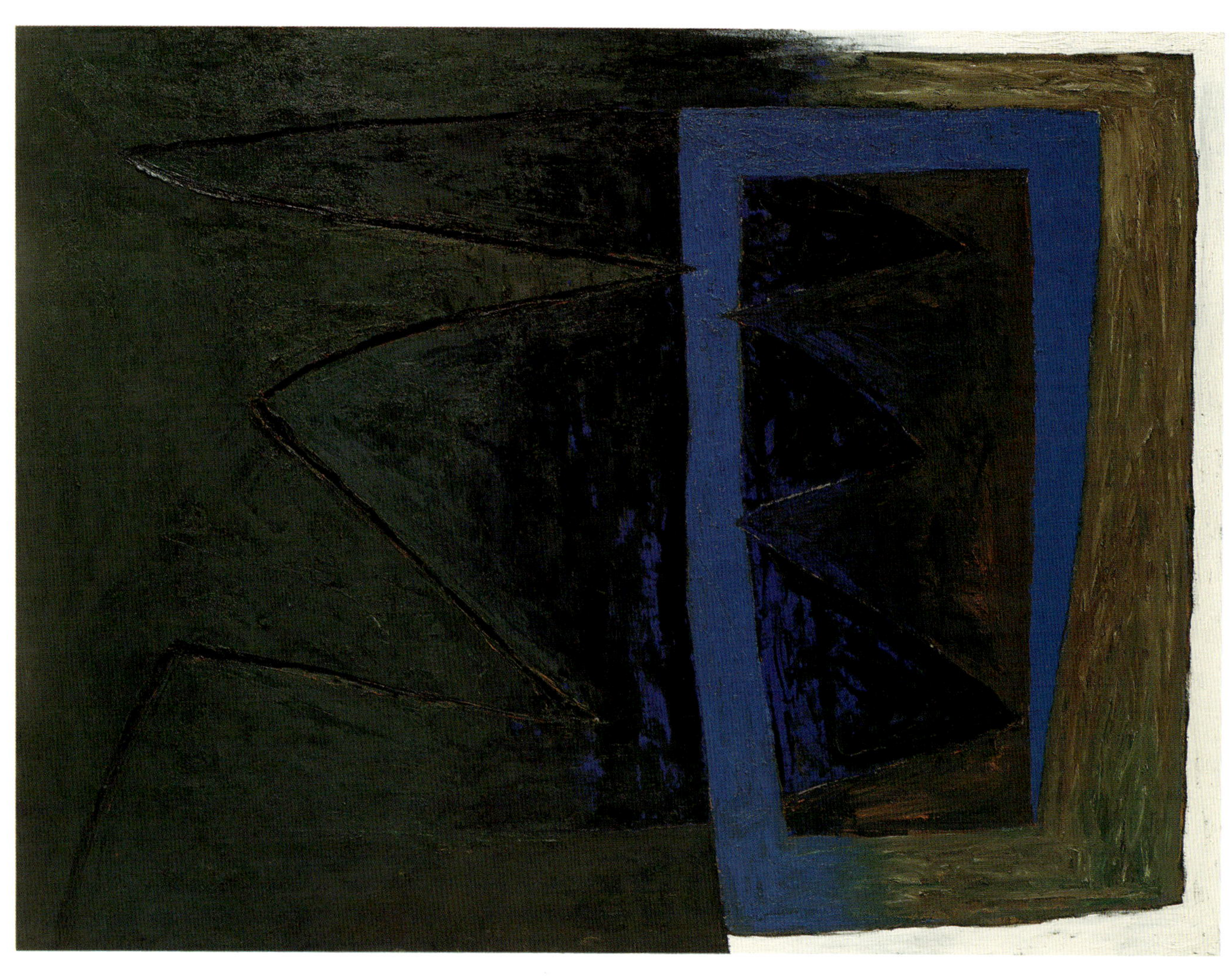

Cat. 5. *The Path to Blue,* 1981, oil on canvas, 67 x 89. Collection of John Deardourff and Elisabeth Griffith

Lenders to the Exhibition

Manfred Baumgartner
Baumgartner Galleries
Best Products Company, Inc.
Murray Bring
Peter Carley
John Deardourff and Elisabeth Griffith
Rosa Esman Gallery
Sandra and James F. Fitzpatrick
George and Betsy Frampton
Sherry Jones and Alan Stone
John Macleod and Ann Klee
The Phillips Collection
Robin Rose and Judith Penski
Ann Willis
William Willis
Private Collections

Foreword

The richly worked surfaces and subtle colors of paintings by artist William Willis contribute to their sense of mystery and inner life. Drawing on the imagery and symbols of diverse cultures, as well as the nature-related forms of the early American modernists, Willis creates an intriguing pictorial language of his own.

This exhibition consists of twenty-eight paintings and works on paper created during the decade 1979–89, with special emphasis on his most recent work. It is particularly appropriate that The Phillips Collection has organized the artist's first extensive solo museum exhibition, since Willis speaks of the influences of many artists he has seen at the Collection.

Organized by Linda L. Johnson, Assistant Curator, with the assistance of Willem de Looper, Consulting Curator, this exhibition is in The Phillips Collection's tradition of encouraging Washington-area artists. We greatly appreciate the generosity of the lenders, as well as the cooperation of Manfred Baumgartner of Baumgartner Galleries, Rosa Esman and Pam Freund of the Rosa Esman Gallery, and the artist himself. On behalf of the curators, I also thank several members of our staff: Joseph Holbach, Registrar; Rebecca Dodson, Assistant Registrar; Patricia Nicholls, Executive Assistant to the Curatorial Department; and William Koberg, Installations Manager.

Laughlin Phillips, Director
The Phillips Collection

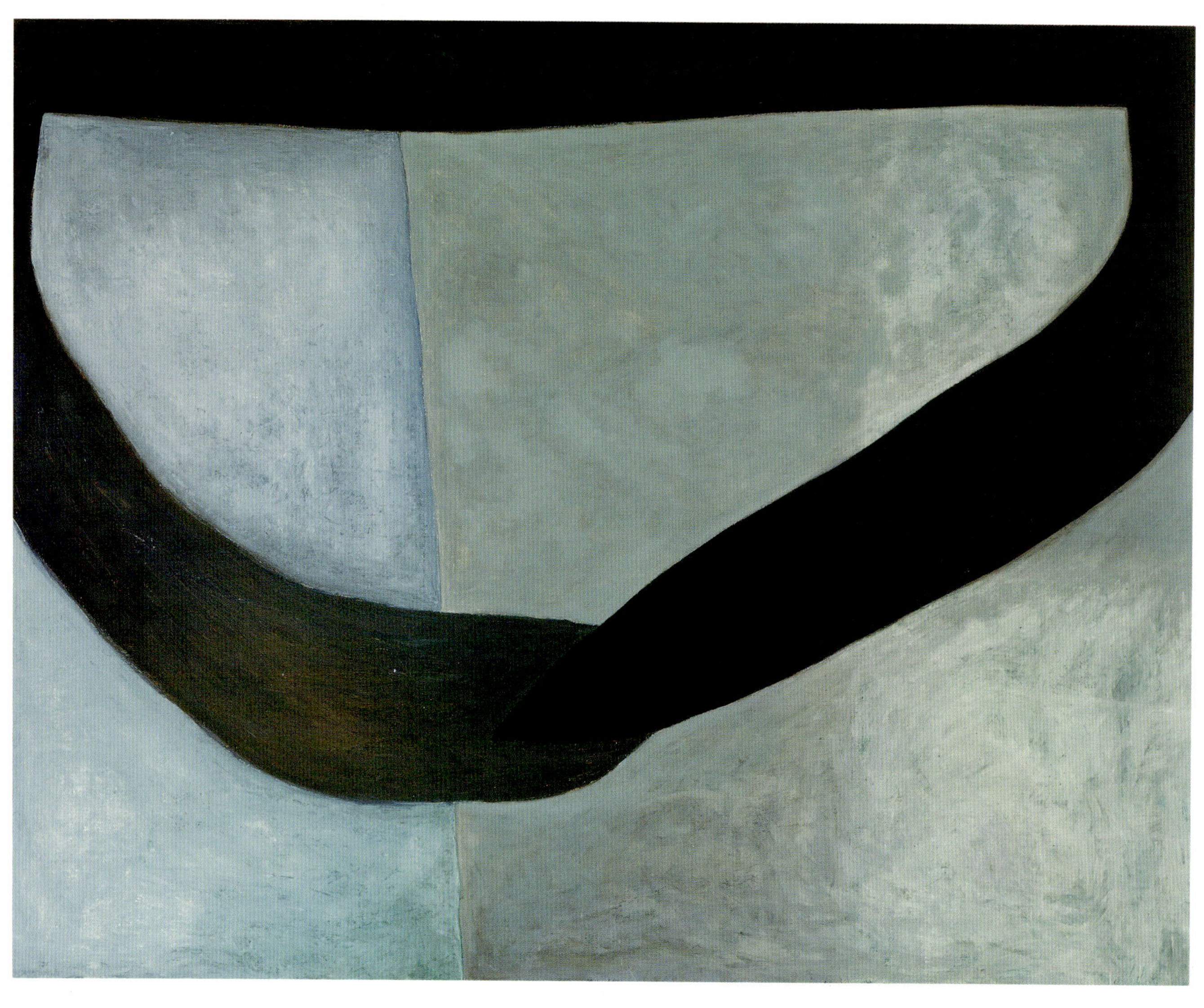

Cat. 9. *The Screen*, 1983, oil on canvas, 88 x 113½. Collection of George and Betsy Frampton

Introduction

Many artists have cited the paintings in The Phillips Collection as important sources of inspiration for their work. There is no other painter that I can think of for whom this connection is more significant than William Willis, who lives and works on the Eastern Shore of Maryland. Willis has regularly shown in Washington and New York during the ten years covered by this exhibition. He has studied and found inspiration in the works of the American modernist artists shown at The Phillips Collection, artists such as Arthur Dove, John Marin, Charles Burchfield, and Marsden Hartley, all of whom Duncan Phillips admired and collected in depth.

Willis' powerful, darkly mysterious, and often quite large paintings are ideally suited to the newly remodeled and much enlarged galleries in The Phillips Collection's annex. In close proximity, one will be able to see some of the many sources that have influenced his work—an abstracted landscape by Dove, a late Philip Guston painting, a small still life by Morandi.

During its more than six decades as a museum of modern art, The Phillips Collection has often presented solo exhibitions of American and European artists at various stages in their development. Most often, these exhibitions have taken place when an artist's work has reached a mature point at which it can be seen in favorable comparison to the works in the permanent collection. In this spirit, the paintings of William Willis are being presented at The Phillips Collection.

Willem de Looper
Consulting Curator

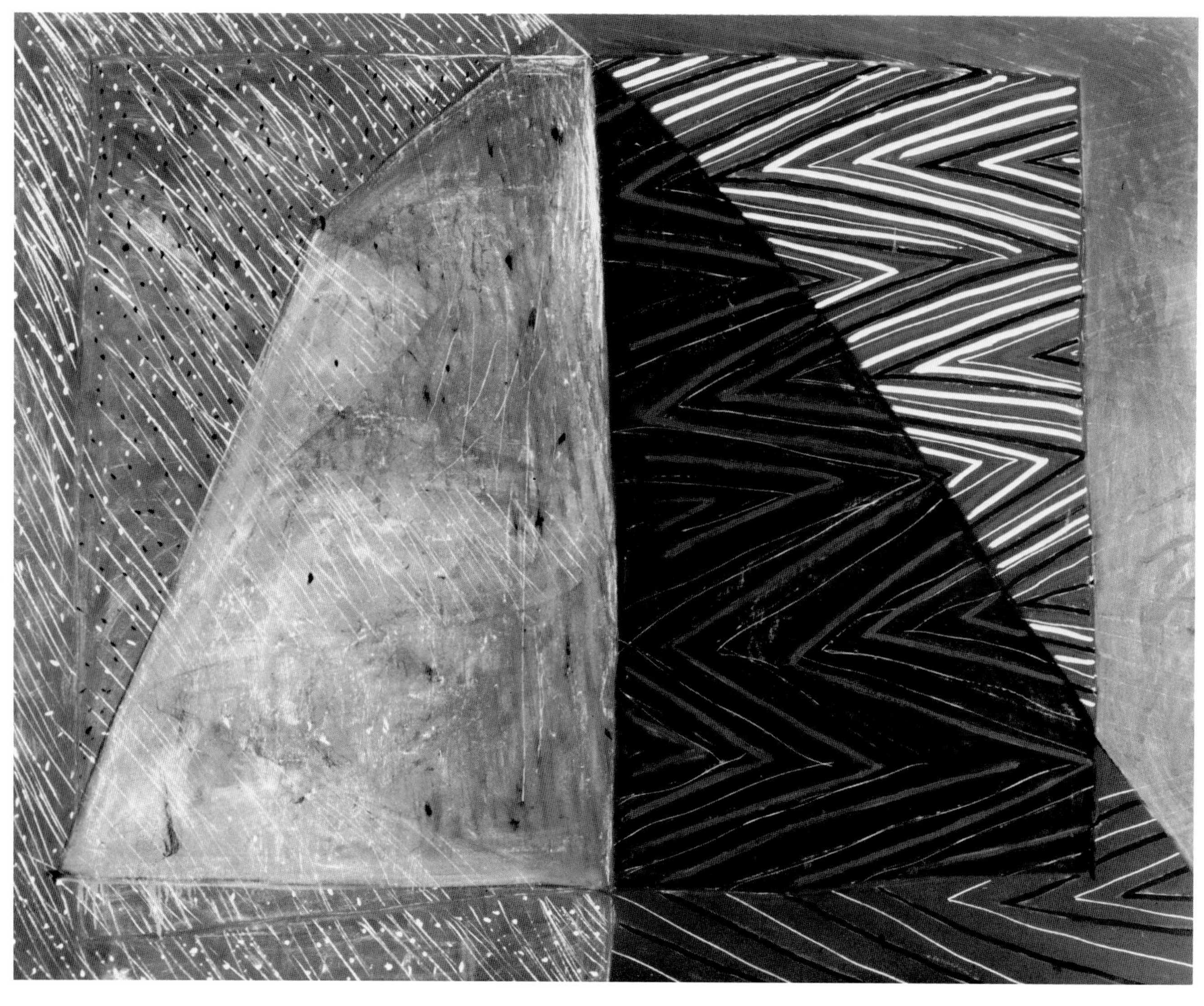

Cat. 2. *Rain Storm for Horace Pippin*, 1979, oil on canvas, 63¼ x 80. Best Products Company, Inc., Richmond, Virginia

William Willis:
Between Moment and Memory

"He who thinks he knows, doesn't know. He who knows that he doesn't know, knows. For in this context, to know is not to know. And not to know is to know." Sanskrit verse[1]

"Painting becomes a tug of war between what you know and what you don't know—between the moment and the pull of memory." Philip Guston[2]

William Willis sees his paintings as vehicles for an immaterial force, a universal, creative source of energy that manifests itself in the material world in a variety of forms, by its very nature evading definition. As Willis has said, "when you categorize art, you don't deal with it. The beauty of art is that it's indefinable and the beauty of this whole thing about approaching that 'source' is its elusiveness. I tell my classes that what we're after is like being in the shower and trying to grab the bar of soap, and the harder you try to grab it, the more it slips away."[3]

Paintings like Willis'—in which shape and meaning shift, slipping in and out of abstraction and representation—elude definition, interpretation, and categorization. His work is difficult to dissect and analyze, knowing how strongly he believes that art should be experienced on a sensory, intuitive, gut level and that categorizing art can strip it of meaning. In response to Heinrich Zimmer, who has described Hindu myths as stories that are "never explained . . . [because] such treatment would sterilize them of their magic," Willis has said, "To explain a picture is worse than to destroy it."[4] This elusiveness is part of the beauty of art—that it cannot always be defined, explained, or put into words. As Kakuzo Okakura has written, when one experiences a powerful work of art, one "catches a glimpse of Infinity, but the words cannot voice his delight, for the eye has no tongue."[5]

Willis' paintings resist explanation as a series of linear, art historical progressions because they keep turning back in on themselves, evading an imposed structure of development. His paintings and their images evolve from one another, each acting as a seed for the next. These evolutions and connections between forms do not usually result from calculated decisions; instead, Willis sees them in retrospect. During the creative process, the images that take shape are intuitive, based on what feels right or makes sense. Only on looking back does he see the evolutionary nature of his work, the chain of relationships that often links his images.

This process of reflection and contemplation is integral to Willis' method of painting, as are a receptivity to chance and discovery and a willingness to let the painting take over at a certain point and paint itself. As the late Philip Guston, an artist Willis admires, once said, "I know that I work in a tension provoked by the contradictions I find in painting. I stay on a picture until a time is reached when these paradoxes vanish and a conscious choice doesn't exist."[6] Willis' work has a cyclical rather than a linear progression that reflects the Hindu tenet that the universe is in a constant cycle of creation, destruction, and reincarnation. His images develop, emerge, lay dormant, and re-

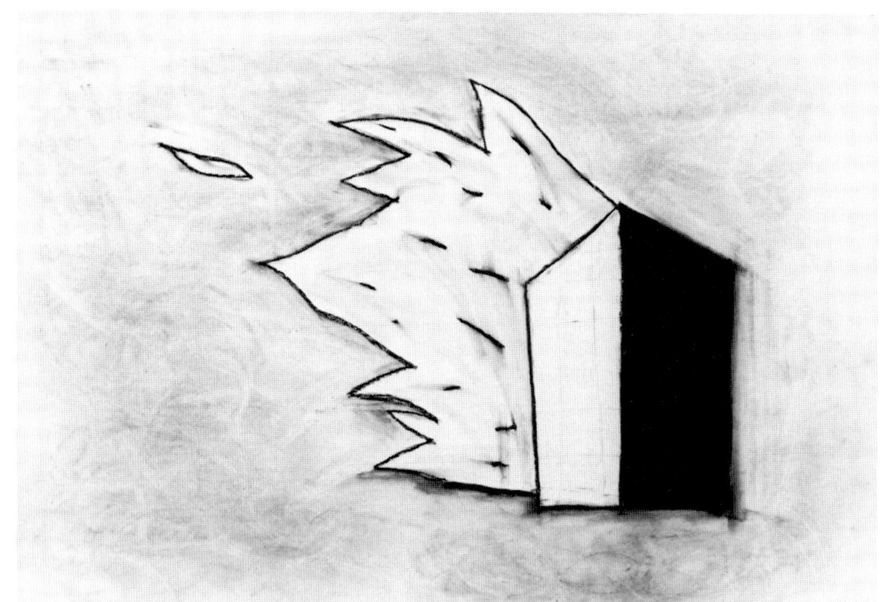

Cat. 3. *Flaming House*, 1981, dirt and charcoal on paper, 26 x 41. Collection of Sherry Jones and Alan Stone, Washington, D.C.

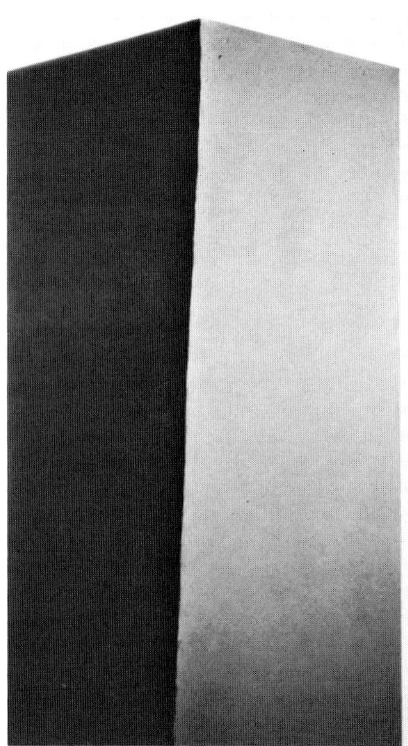

Fig. 1. William Willis, *House*, 1979, acrylic on canvas, 85 x 49. Courtesy of Baumgartner Galleries, Washington, D.C., and Rosa Esman Gallery, New York

surface in different forms, in keeping with his belief in the interconnectedness and interweaving of all things in the world.

The images in Willis' paintings are born out of a melding of many influences and personal interests. He has been influenced by other artists, including Charles Burchfield, Giorgio Morandi, Philip Guston, Georges Braque, and Horace Pippin. His work refers to the symbols and myths of India and Egypt, the traditional arts of Japan and the American Indians, and the philosophies of Zen Buddhism, Hinduism, and Christianity. Willis gathers, assimilates, and transforms elements from these diverse sources to create his own evocative pictorial language. Infused with meaning, metaphor, memory, symbol, and association, his paintings tap into a universal source that transcends the material world. Willis strives to put into paint his sense of the world and hopes that if he does it well enough, the intensity of his vision will communicate on its own terms, moving the viewer beyond the physical image.

Willis works with a consistent vocabulary of images that he has gradually built up over the years. The evolution of one of his images begins, for example, with a minimal house shape in *Hyena* (1977, cat. 1) and *House* (1979, fig. 1). The image then becomes a house on fire in *Flaming House* (1981, cat. 3), the jagged flames of which relate back to a zig-zag pattern in *Rain Storm for Horace Pippin* (1979, cat. 2). This jagged shape in turn evolves into the zig-zag or thunderbolt shape in *The Path to Blue* (1981, cat. 5) and then resurfaces as a tree in *Falling Tree* (1982, cat. 7), becoming the mouth of a fish in *The Garden* (1985–87, cat. 14). Most recently, the zig-zag image appeared as the shape formed by the angles of a folded screen in *Haṁ Sa (The Gander)* (1989, cat. 28).

Edge of Influence (1978–85, cat. 11) is a painting that Willis worked and reworked over eight years, throughout most of these transformations. It captures the essence of the jagged zig-zag shape as a symbol for creative energy in its abstracted and concen-

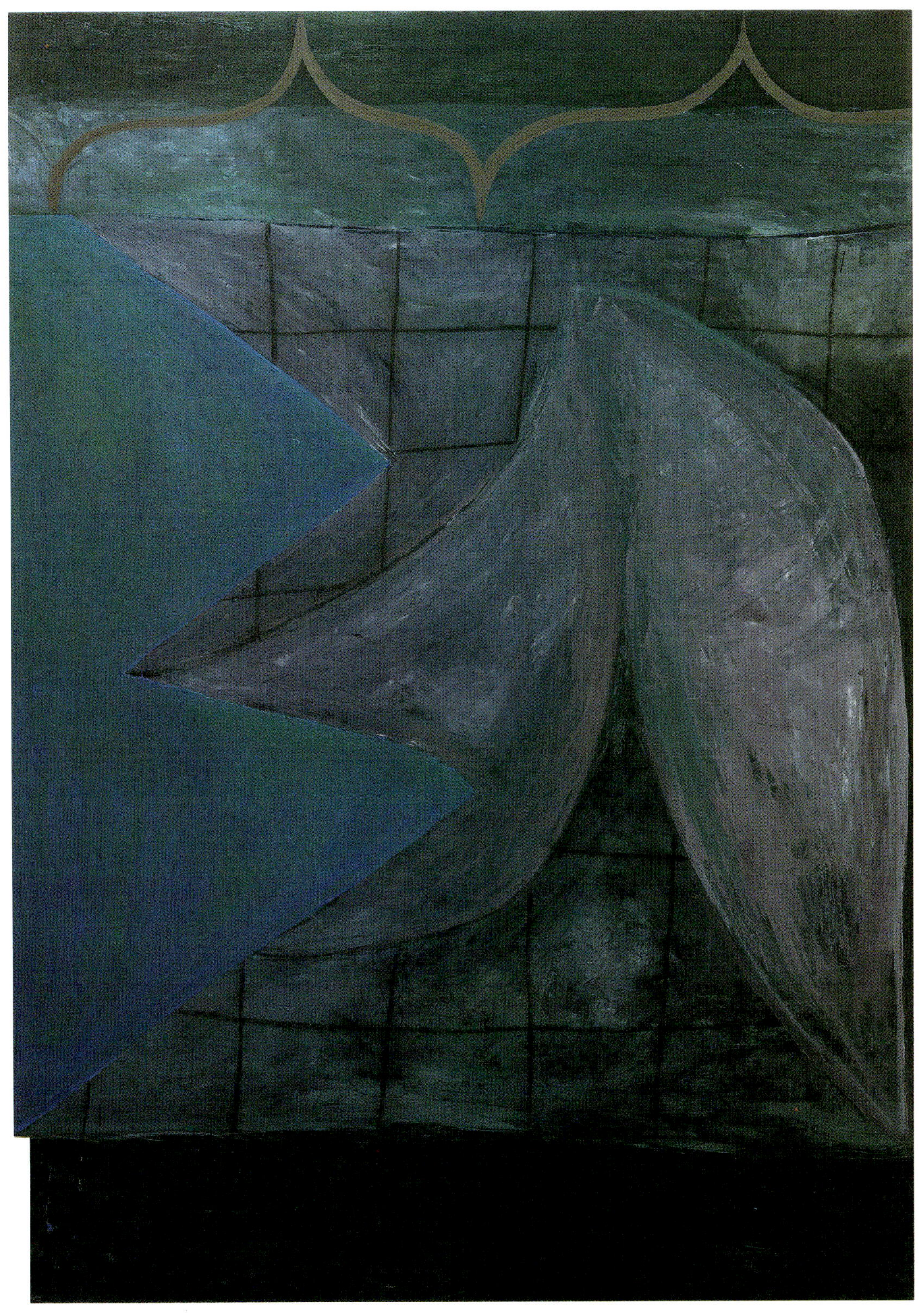

Cat. 14. *The Garden*, 1985-87, oil on canvas, 86 x 62½. Collection of Manfred Baumgartner

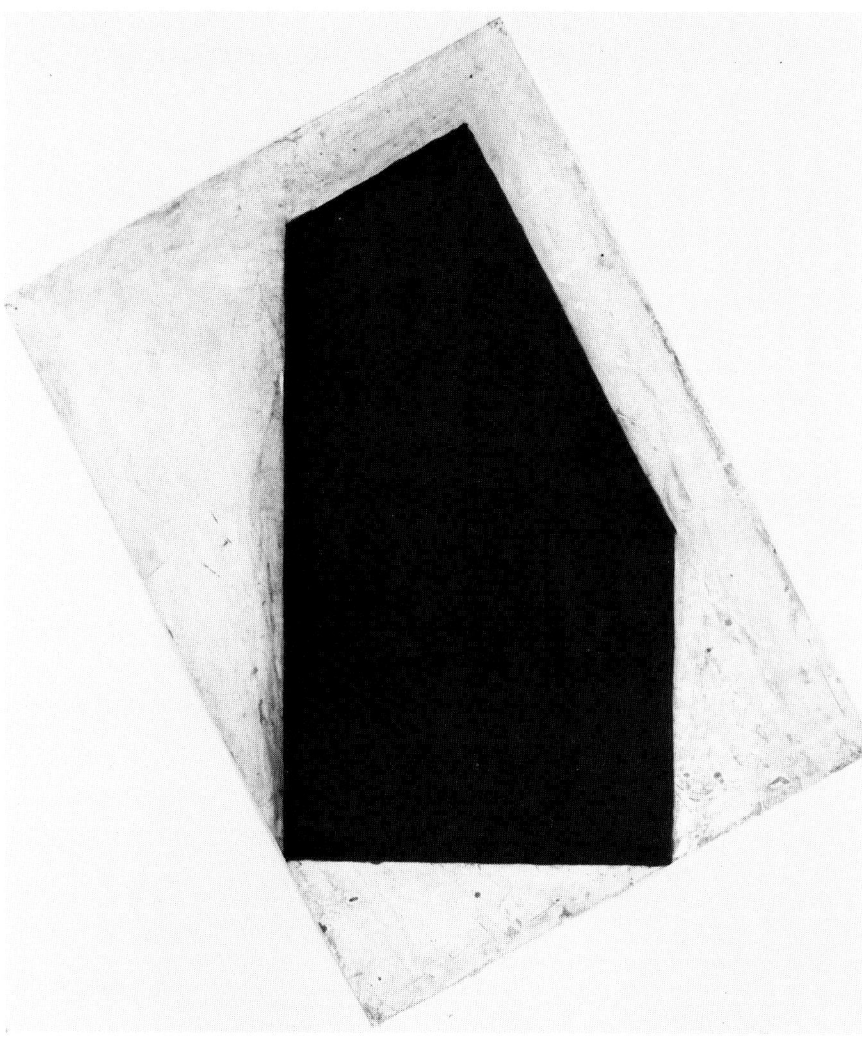

Cat. 1. *Hyena*, 1977, oil on gessoed paper, 50½ x 44¼. The Phillips Collection, Washington, D.C. Gift of Mr. John Naisbitt and Ms. Patricia Aburdene, 1989

trated form, composed of vertical and horizontal bands that lock the picture in. The zig-zag shape grew out of a variety of sources—lightning bolts, the shape formed by the artist's initials, WW, linked together, the decorative patterns of Navaho rugs and pottery. These references are melded and synthesized into images that are not literal symbols, but are there because they are the forms that work, that make sense, that have personal meaning for Willis.

The screen is another recurring image in Willis' paintings, as in *The Screen* (1983, cat. 9) and *Untitled (Blue Screen)* (1988, cat. 22). The image of the screen later evolves into an open book in *Untitled (Ledger)* (1988, cat. 25) and *Untitled (Flyby)* (1988–89, cat. 27) and resurfaces as a screen in *Haṁ Sa (The Gander)* (1989, cat. 28). Shapes of pyramids and triangles from works of the late 1970s—such as *Bushmaster* (1979, fig. 2) and *Rain Storm for Horace Pippin* (1979, cat. 2) —reemerged in the 1980s in the form of a Hindu symbol, the yoni, as in *Untitled (Black Lingam)* (1983–84, cat. 10).

In the late 1970s, Willis' paintings concentrated on images that, although minimal in form and color, are also evocative and referential. Flat, monochromatic, and close to the surface, the forms in works such as *Hyena* (1977, cat. 1), *House* (1979, fig. 1), and *Bushmaster* (1979, fig. 2), are simple and geometric. Willis has described the process of creating these early works as "skinning a painting like a rabbit," paring an image down to its essence by carving out the unessential.[7] In *Hyena*, the house shape loses its identity as a symbol of stability and becomes an unsettling image. The paper it is centered on is mounted at an angle, dangling precariously within the frame (the posi-

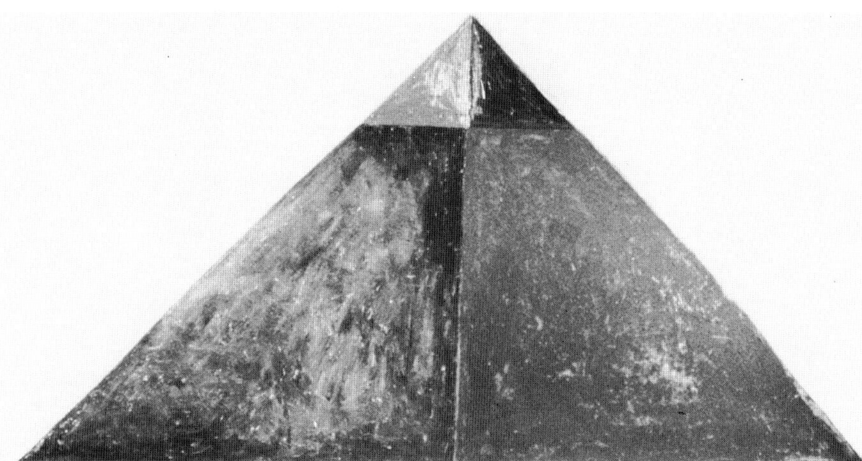

Fig. 2. William Willis, *Bushmaster*, 1979, oil on canvas, 66 x 120. Courtesy of Baumgartner Galleries, Washington, D.C., and Rosa Esman Gallery, New York

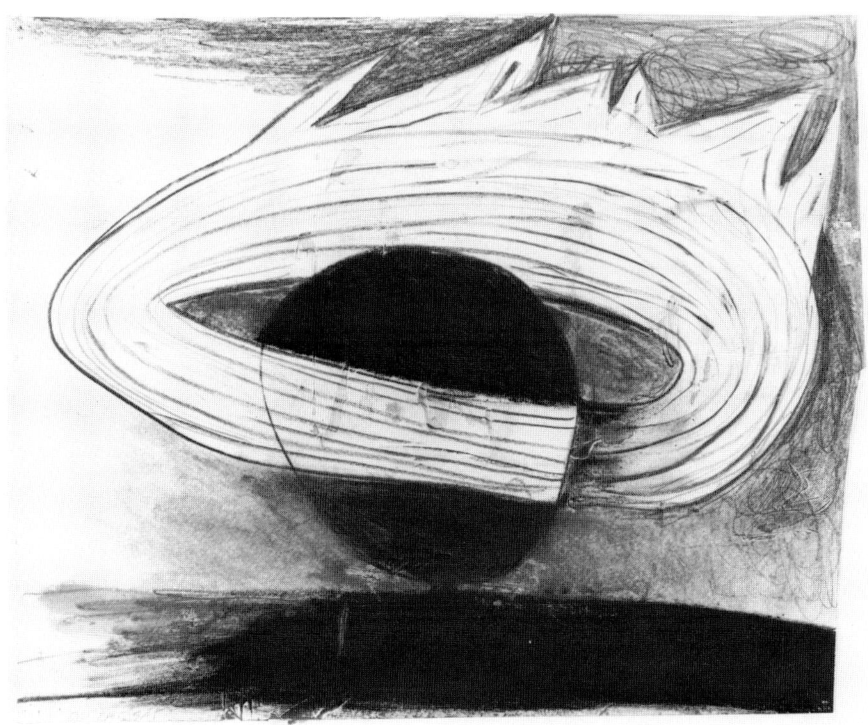

Cat. 16. *Saturn*, 1987, charcoal, pencil, and gouache on paper, 22 x 29. Collection of Robin Rose and Judith Penski

tion the paper fell into when one of the staples that held it to the wall fell out while Willis was working on it), and the shape of the house itself is disquieting in its asymmetry. The title refers to an animal whose back legs are much shorter than its front legs, like the disturbing proportions of this house.

In 1981, the house reappeared in *Flaming House* (cat. 3), a work in which the basic house form is taken beyond the minimal geometry of the previous works to create a compelling image of a house on fire. Playing with duality and polarity, the stark black and white image of a divided house is set in an atmospheric, seductive gray field that was created by rubbing dirt into the paper. *Flaming House* is a primal, archetypal image that in its austerity and simplicity has the power to imprint itself on one's mind, enduring and persisting long after one leaves the work behind.

Willis has described 1979 as a pivotal year in his work, a time in which he was taking in and trying out different images; reading about and becoming more involved with yoga, mythology, and religion; and looking at traditional arts and the work of other artists. *Rain Storm for Horace Pippin* (1979, cat. 2) was inspired in part by an exhibition of Pippin's work that Willis had seen at The Phillips Collection in 1977. With this painting, Willis began to move away from the simple geometry of the previous works toward more complex images. He started with a basic pyramid shape that he had used earlier and added to it by dividing the canvas into layered sections of overlapping shapes. Unlike his earlier works, this abstracted landscape concentrates on detail and pattern to animate the surface of the painting, reflecting both his interest in the geometric patterns found in American Indian art and the influence

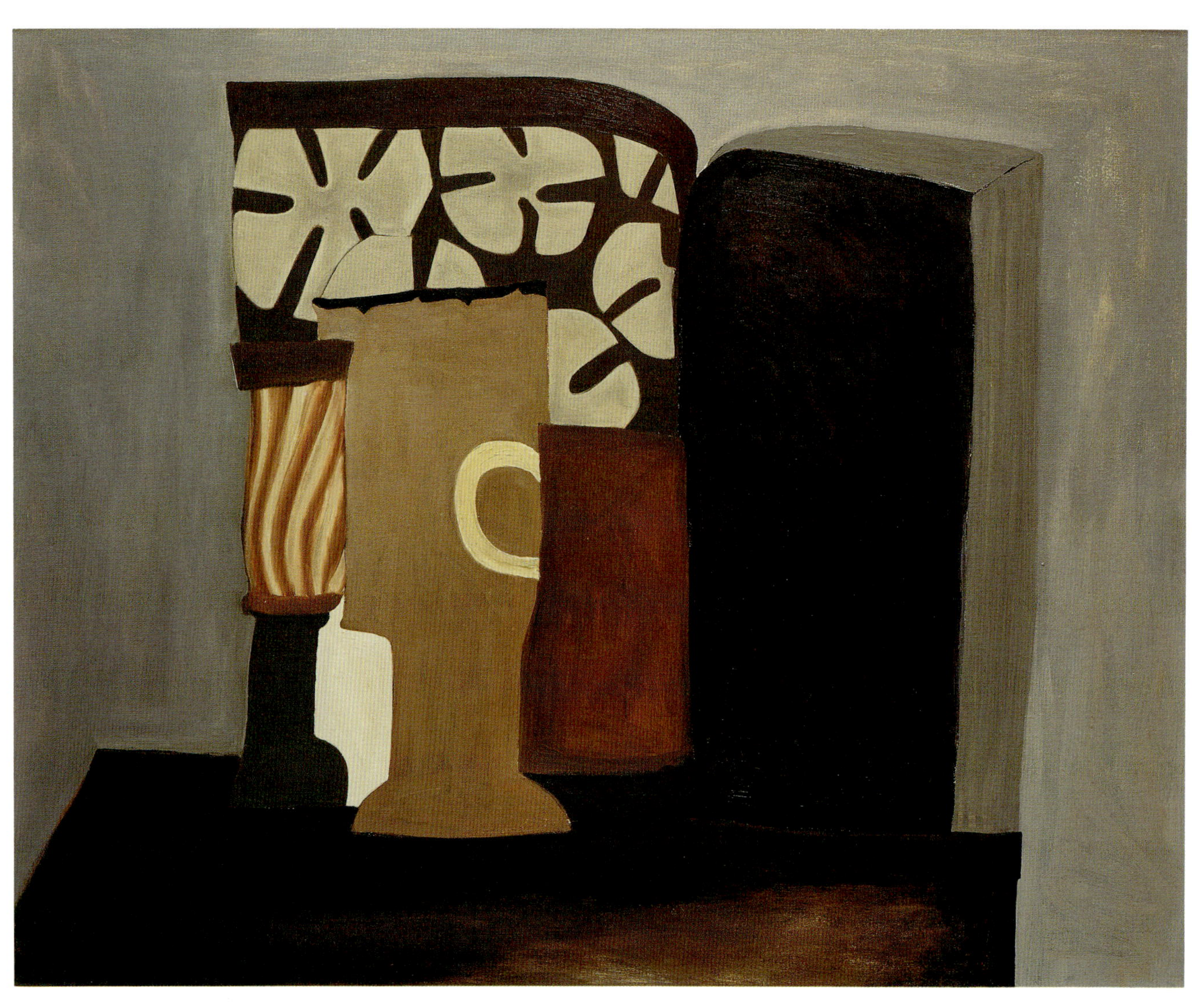

Cat. 21. *Heroes,* 1988, oil on canvas, 38 x 48. Courtesy of Baumgartner Galleries, Washington, D.C., and Rosa Esman Gallery, New York

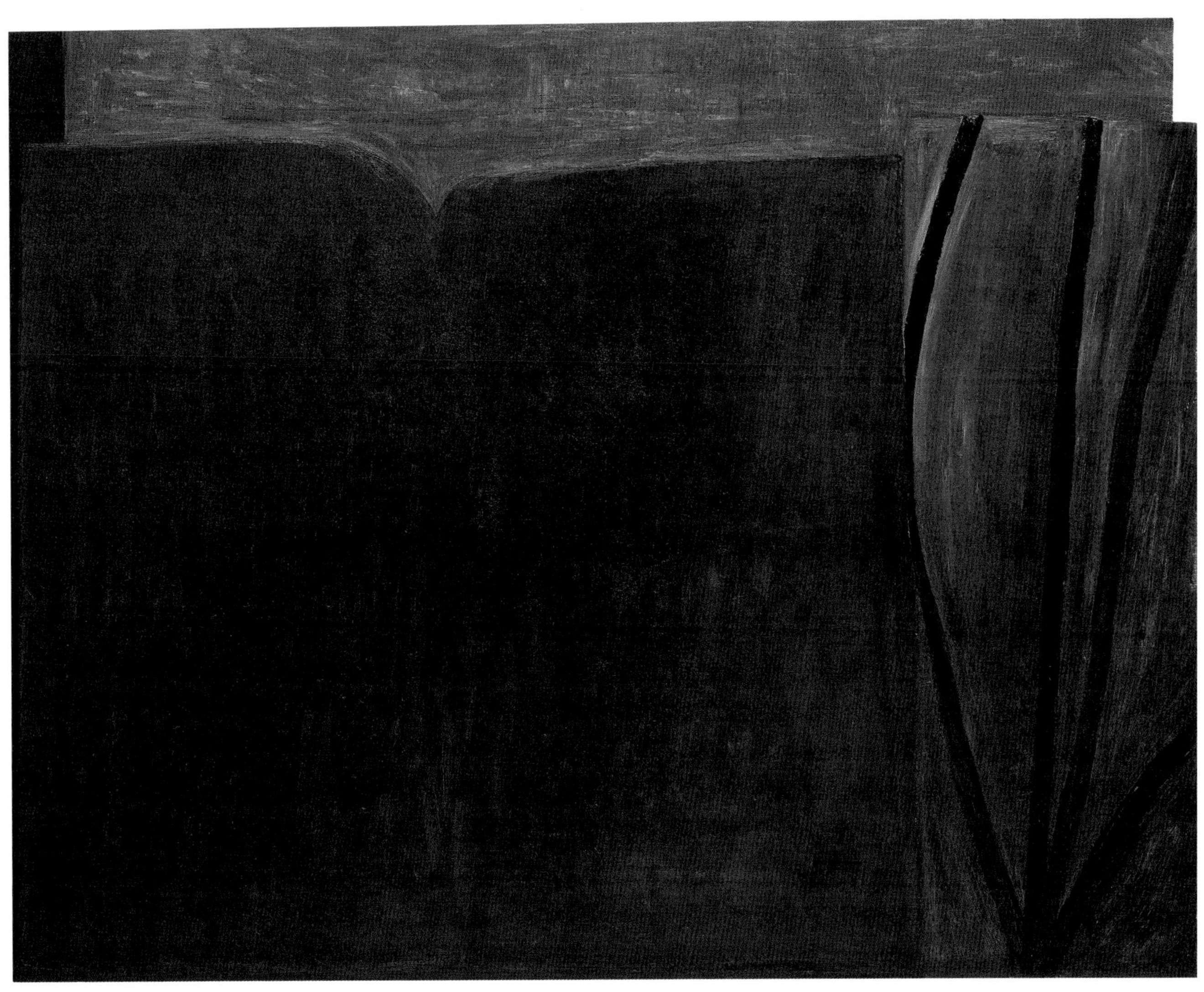

Cat. 25. *Untitled (Ledger)*, 1988, oil on canvas, 68½ x 88½. Courtesy of Baumgartner Galleries, Washington, D.C., and Rosa Esman Gallery, New York

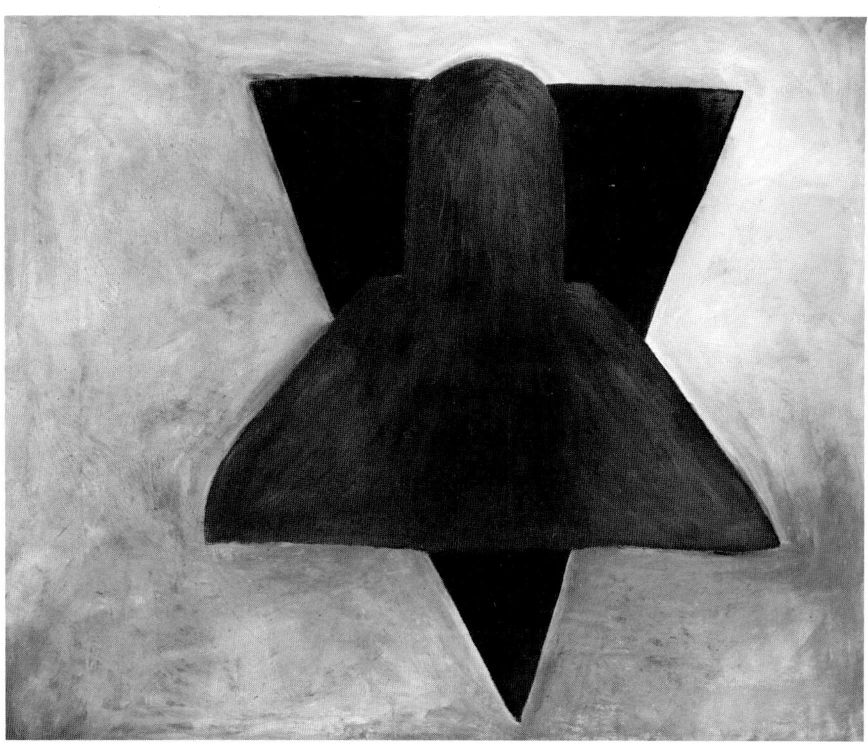

Fig. 3. William Willis, *Untitled (Avadhoota)*, 1985-87, oil on canvas, 84½ x 103. Collection of the artist

Fig. 4. William Willis, *Fish with Śrī-Yantra*, 1984, oil on canvas, 41 x 60. Collection of the artist

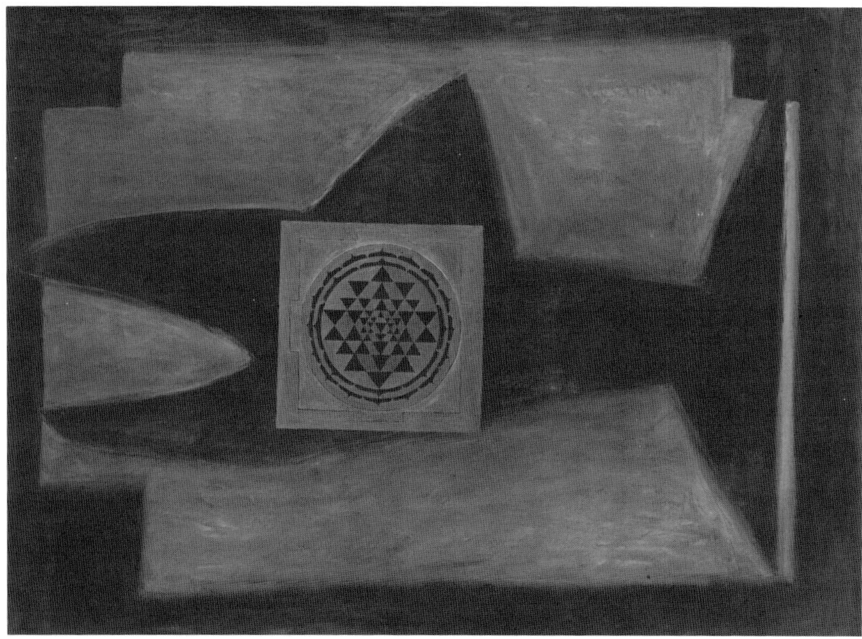

of the short, sharp, linear brushstrokes that create movement across the picture plane in Pippin's landscapes to give the feeling of a storm.

In the 1970s, Willis often began a work by painting a grid on the canvas, filling in each unit of the grid with Xs, and then painting it out. The grid became the underlying structure that held the painting together, but it was also something to paint over and get rid of, a way to get a painting started. Eventually, Willis began to see other geometrical shapes within the grid—the asymmetrical pentagonal shape in *Hyena*, the triangular shapes in *Bushmaster* and *Rain Storm for Horace Pippin*—and the grid itself became a less dominant element. The grid still surfaces occasionally in Willis' recent work, as in the background of *The Garden* (1985–87, cat. 14), scratched into the surface and veiled by layers of paint in *Untitled (Kalaśa)* (1986–88, cat. 19), and in *Haṁ Sa (The Gander)* (1989, cat. 28). In these works, the grid also stands for an Eastern concept of the universe, in which, as Willis describes it, "everything is basically part of one big divine pattern or grid."[8]

Willis has been interested in Eastern philosophy and religion since he was introduced to Zen concepts through the art of Jasper Johns and Robert Rauschenberg as a student in the 1960s and 1970s. But until the late 1970s, he had only pursued this interest in theory. In 1979, a friend took him to a meditation center, introducing him to what would become an ongoing involvement in yoga and meditation, and he began to practice the concepts that had always intrigued him on an intellectual level.

During the early 1980s, Willis' painting was closely connected to his involvement in yoga and the philosophies and teachings of Swami Muktananda, whom he first met in 1980. At this time, he was consciously making art that paid homage to a spiritual source. Referring back to this period, Willis recently said, "I remember

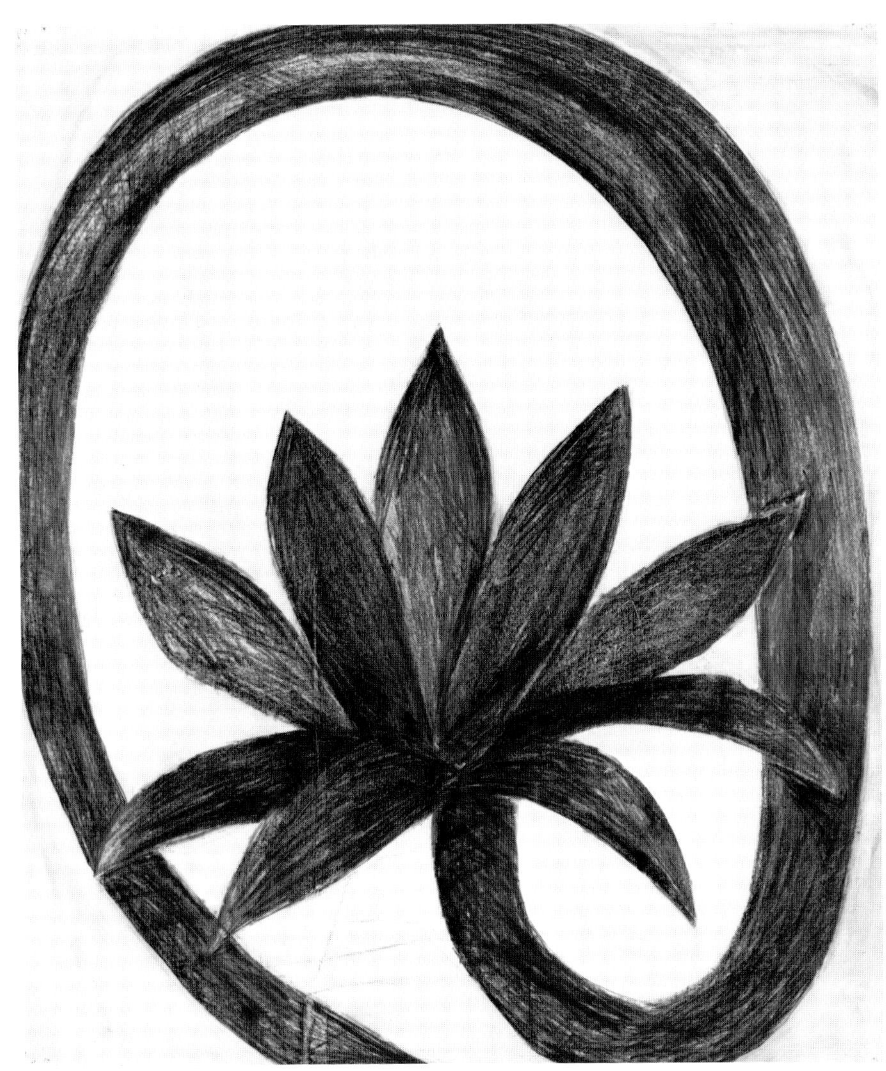

Cat. 13. *Untitled (Lotus)*, 1986, pencil and gesso on paper, 25 x 21¾. Collection of Ann Willis

writing in my notebook one day that all I wanted to do was do paintings for God, Shiva, whatever you want to call it, and do them in that traditional sense of these classic symbols of the lingam and the yantra."[9] But he later realized that painting these literal symbols was not enough, that he is an American artist painting in the twentieth-century, and he could only admire, not emulate, the traditional Indian craftsmen of the past who created religious works of art for meditation and worship.

Willis' work is often discussed in terms of its "spiritual" nature, a category he strongly resists because he feels that it is restricting and misleading: "I'm not so interested in religion as I'm interested in what religion itself is ultimately interested in: the source of religion. What I'm really interested in is the underlying element that [fuels] all religions, . . . the fact that there is some kind of sense of creative energy, some sense of interconnectedness of everything, [a force] that transcends religion—that's what [all religion is ultimately about] and that is also what art is about."[10]

Willis' paintings are not about Eastern symbols and religions. The images he employs do not have specific meanings attached. But Hindu symbols are the focus of many of his works of the mid– to late 1980s. In *Untitled (Black Lingam)* (1983–84, cat. 10) and *Untitled (Avadhoota)* (1985–87, fig. 3), the triangular forms represent the yoni, the Hindu symbol for the feminine, and the phallic forms are the lingam, the masculine symbol. *Fish with Śrī-Yantra* (1984, fig. 4) incorporates the circular form of a mandala or yantra, an intricate, geometric pattern that serves as an aid to concentration while meditating. The lotus appears in several of Willis'

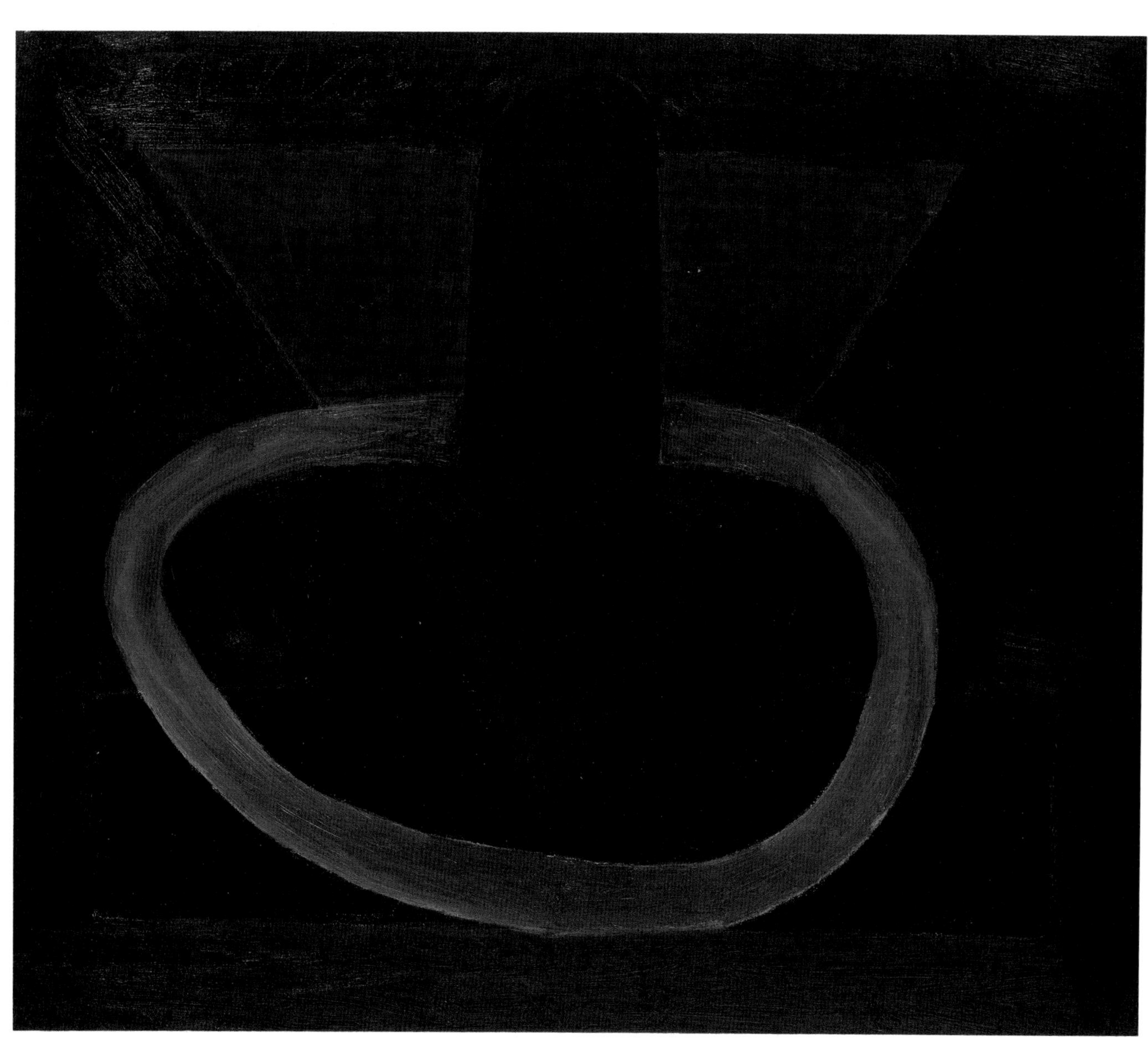

Cat. 10. *Untitled (Black Lingam)*, 1983-84, oil on canvas, 26 x 30. Collection of Sandra and James F. Fitzpatrick

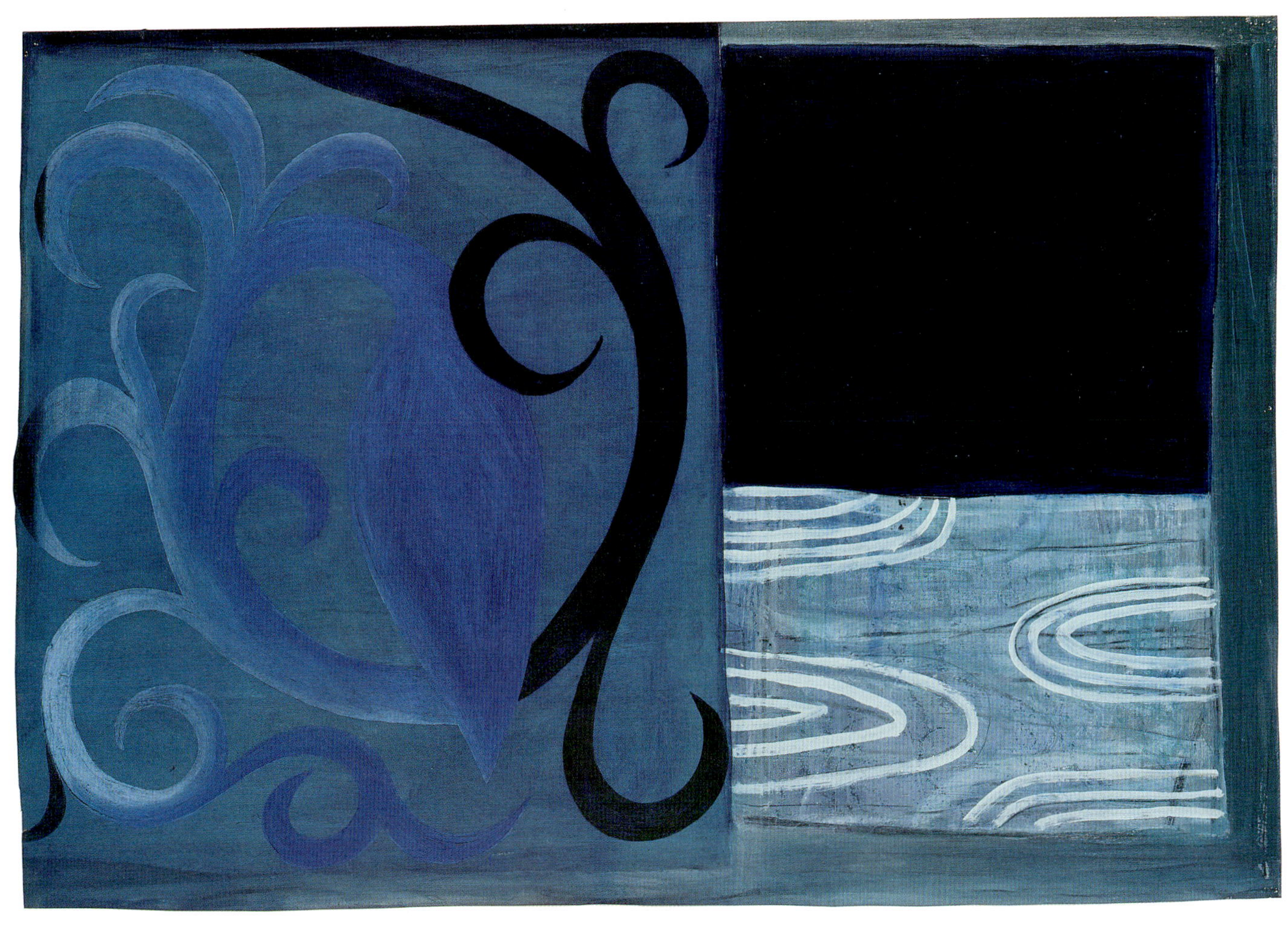

Cat. 22. *Untitled (Blue Screen)*, 1988, oil on gessoed paper, 31 x 45¾. Collection of John Macleod and Ann Klee

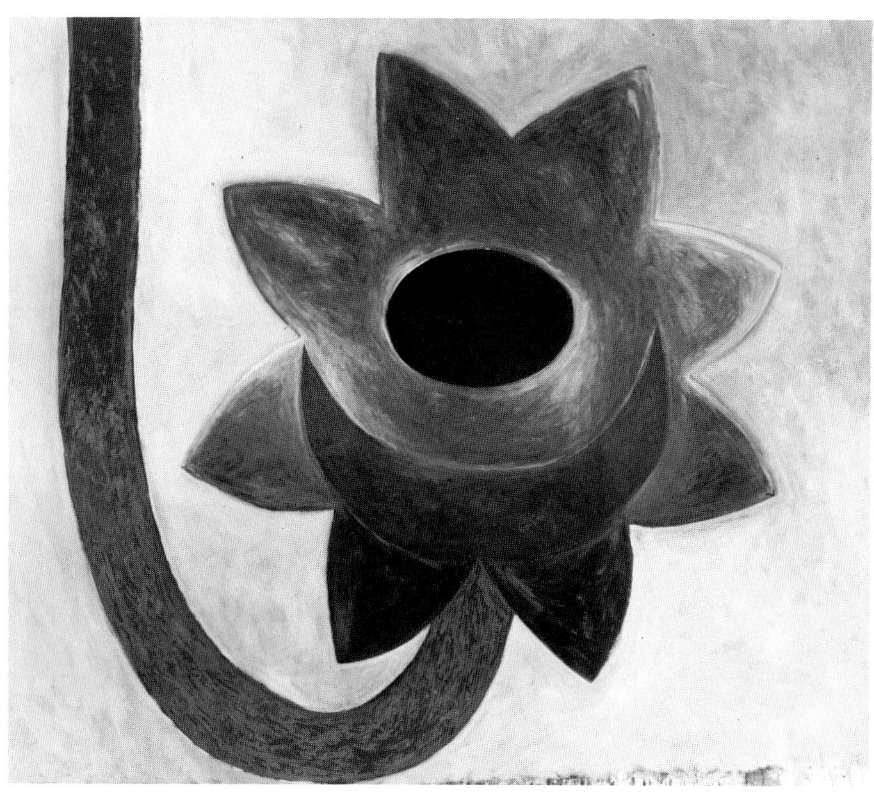

Fig. 5. William Willis, *The Source*, 1985, oil on canvas, 84 x 103. Collection of the artist

works, including *Untitled (Lotus)* (1986, cat. 13), *The Source* (1985, fig. 5), and *Screen with Lotus* (1978–88, cat. 18). The lotus is a life-giving source symbolizing creation and birth in Indian art and mythology, but it also represents the Eastern concept of the universal coexistence of good and evil, in that the lotus is a divine form that rises out of the murky depths of a pond.[11] In Willis' recent work, the lotus has appeared in a more stylized form, as in the decorative pattern that covers a vase in *Heroes* (1988, cat. 21).

When Willis was painting works with such obvious religious symbols, it was difficult not to latch on to them as a way to understand his work. As Douglas Greenwood wrote in a 1988 review, "In Willis' view, eastern religions provide one central way of articulating truth, of providing information. Each religion has its own symbols, its own values, none of them any more or less valid than another. Yet because he consistently deals with eastern or oriental images, people unfamiliar with the iconography may miss the 'point' of his art. As he puts it: 'Culture is like a vehicle. Whether it's a Chevrolet or a Mercedes, the goal is [to] get where you're going.' He adds, 'I have no problem using whatever transportation is around.' "[12]

Like the metaphors employed in myths, the images of Willis' paintings are not meant to be interpreted literally. Instead, they are intended to be the catalysts to something that lies beyond the image. And as in myths, the point is lost if one tries to understand Willis' images at face value. As Joseph Campbell has described the use of metaphors in myths, "The images are outward, but their reflection is inward. . . . When your mind is simply trapped by the image out there so that you never make the reference to yourself, you have misread the image."[13] And as Willis has said, "Identifying with a symbol or an image is also a kind of screen that keeps you away from experiencing the very thing that's there, call it spiritual or whatever—that very source of the act of painting or creativity."[14] The shapes Willis uses, he says, "just represent . . . that creative energy, that source of everything. So it's my way very humbly of trying to pay homage to that aspect of existence that makes all this."[15]

Willis inscribes a mantra on all of his works, sometimes on the front, but usually on the back: "Om Tat Sat," or "I pay homage to that source from which I come." In *Untitled (Flyby)* (1988–89, cat. 27), an inscription on the book in the background, "Om Namah Shivaya," loosely translates as "I bow to the inner Self." Although this source is much too elusive to be completely captured in a

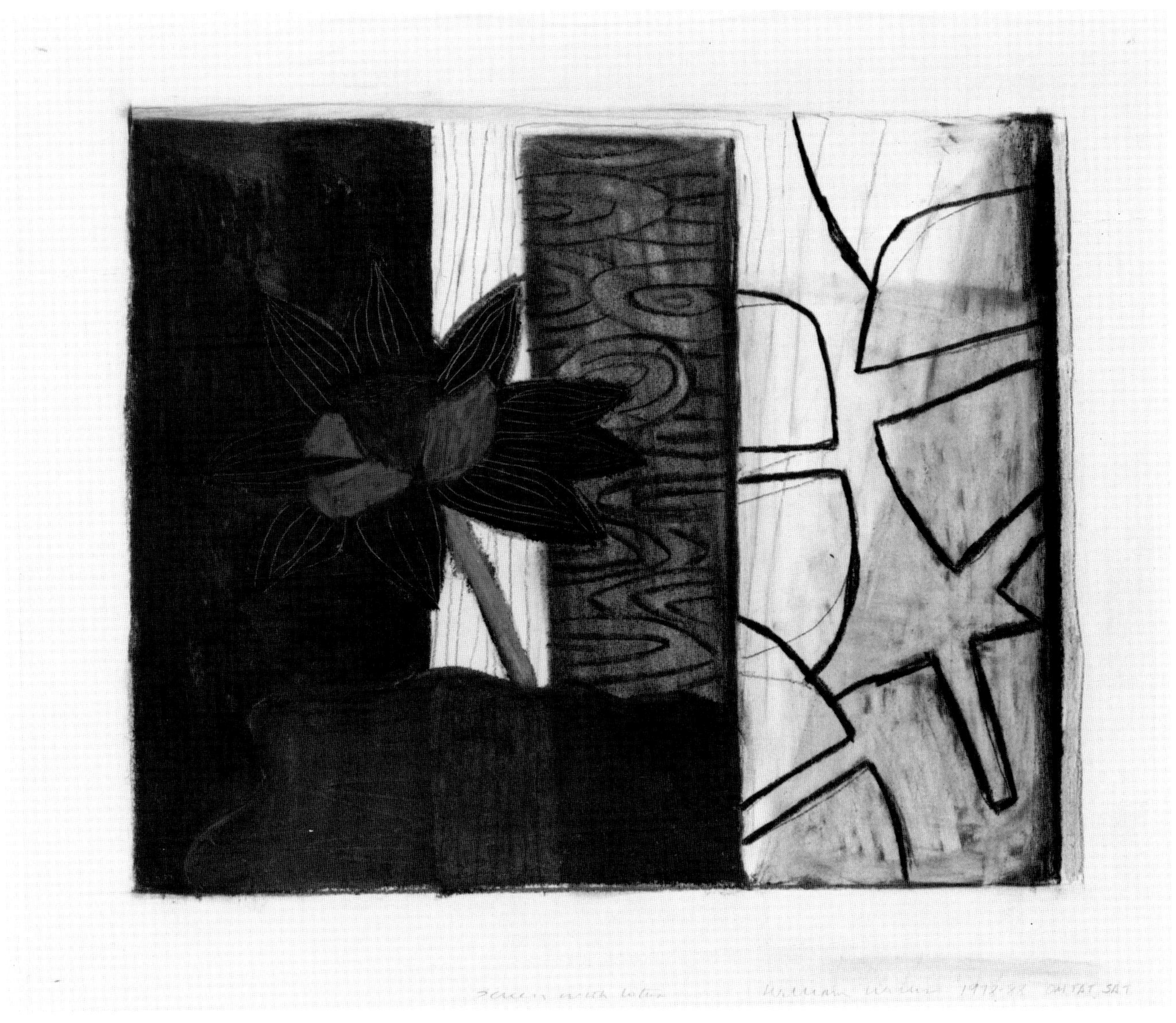

Cat. 18. *Screen with Lotus*, 1978-88, pencil, charcoal, and oil pastel on paper, 14 x 16½. Collection of the artist

material form, the painting can act as the jumping-off point, the impetus that will get one to something beyond the physical picture. The Hindu term for this source is shakti, the cosmic energy that is the creative force behind everything, "the power inherent in cause to produce its necessary effect."[16]

In recent works, such as *Untitled (Kalaśa)* (1986–88, cat. 19) and *Haṁ Sa (The Gander)* (1989, cat. 28), the Eastern sources and spiritual references are more symbolic than representational, more metaphoric than literal. The meanings are harder to get at, but the paintings are more powerful and lasting because of their ambiguity and hidden content. *Haṁ Sa (The Gander)* is composed of two elementary images: a bird and a folding screen. Minimal, unadorned, devoid of detail, it consists of simple, overlapping shapes that form a grid of horizontals and verticals, a device that Willis frequently uses to anchor the composition into the picture plane. The bright, white wings of the bird cut

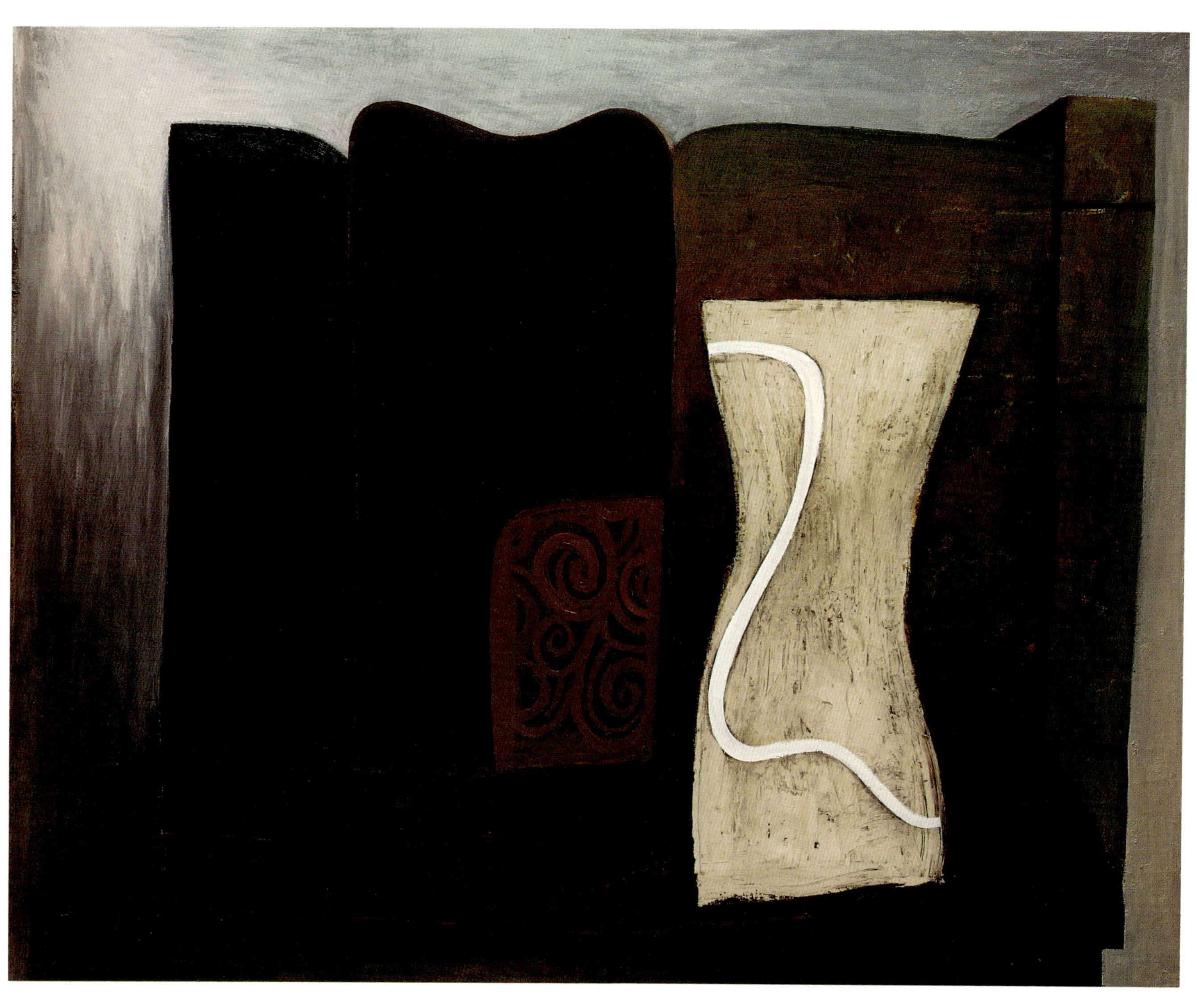

Cat. 19. *Untitled (Kalaśa)*, 1986-88, oil on canvas, 86 x 109¼. Courtesy of Baumgartner Galleries, Washington, D.C., and Rosa Esman Gallery, New York

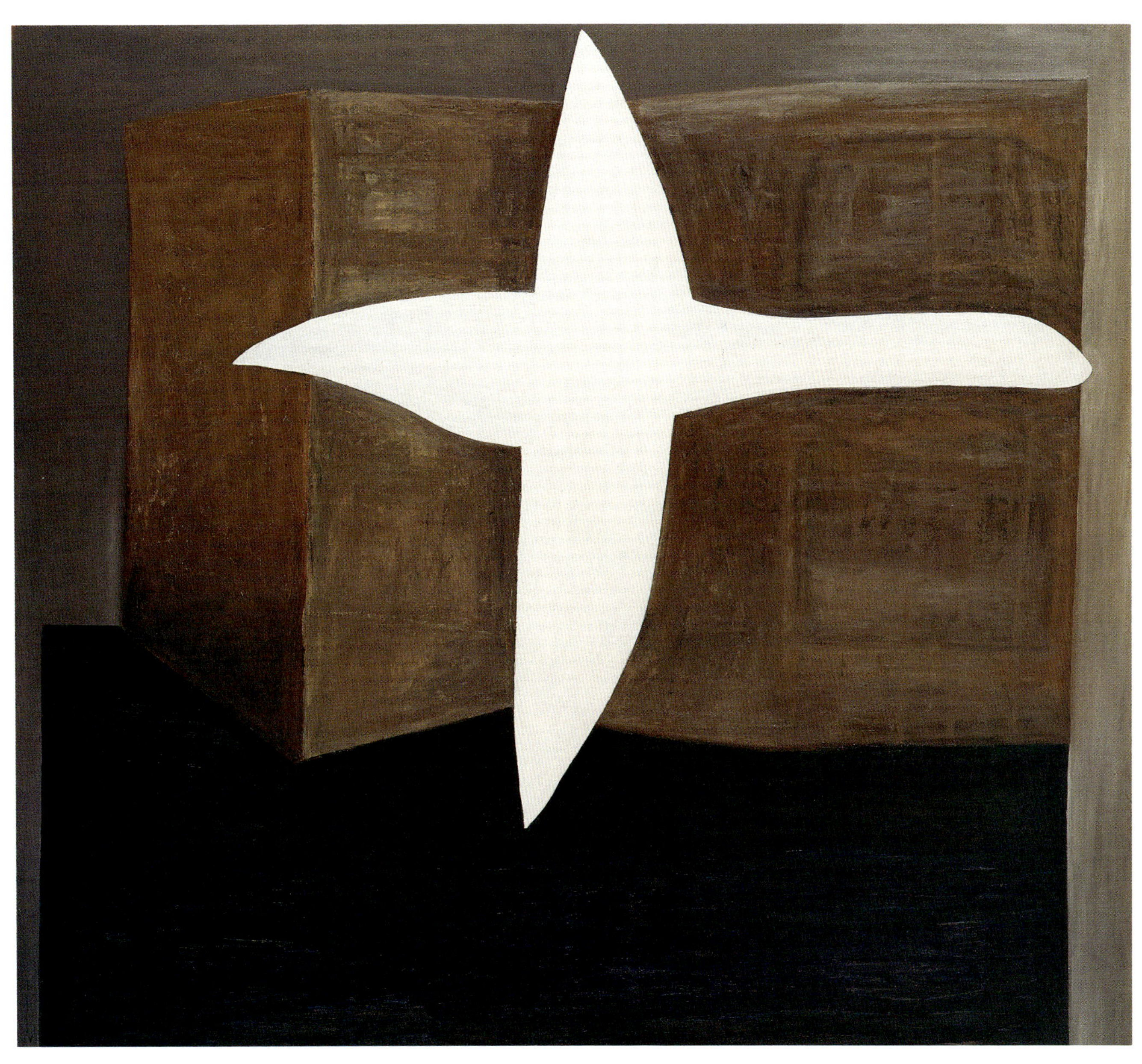

Cat. 28. *Haṁ Sa (The Gander)*, 1989, oil on canvas, 75 x 88. Courtesy of Baumgartner Galleries, Washington, D.C., and Rosa Esman Gallery, New York

into the canvas, bisecting the space. The luminescent bird pushes forward, expanding into the space beyond the canvas, as the dark colors of the background recede. Like Braque's birds (see fig. 12), the bird in *Haṁ Sa (The Gander)* is an emblematic, iconic image, rather than a depiction of a specific bird.

Haṁ Sa (The Gander) can be read on multiple levels, alluding to a variety of sources. The image of the bird refers to the wild geese that Willis sees on the Eastern Shore of Maryland where he lives and to Braque's abstracted birds. It also relates to the Hindu myth of the wild gander, Haṁ Sa, one of the many forms in which Vishnu, the Supreme Being, appears. "Ham sa, sa ham," the melody created by the bird's breathing, translates as "I am this, this am I," which means "I, the human individual—actually and fundamentally am This, or He, namely the Self, the Highest Being."[17] The gander symbolizes both the universal source of energy and the duality of all beings; everything is of both worlds, spiritual and material, dark and light, good and evil. Haṁ Sa "swims on the surface of the water, but is not bound to it. Withdrawing from the watery realm, it wings into the pure and stainless air, where it is as much at home as in the world below. . . . This is the boundless free wanderer, between the upper celestial and the lower earthly spheres, at ease in both, not bound to either."[18]

On top of these universal references and associations, Willis often layers autobiographical content. *The Screen* (1983, cat. 9) combines childhood memories of catching snakes in the Florida swamps with references to the image of a snake biting its tail—a symbol for the eternal cycle of creation and destruction which appears in the myths of many cultures. The painting's title refers to a line from a yoga text that Swami Muktaṇanda quotes in his writings: "She unfolds this universe upon Her own screen."[19]

These complex associations with myth and symbol clearly demonstrate that Willis' images are not just based on individual experiences. They are archetypal images that dredge up meaning and connections from a universal subconcious. As Joseph Campbell has observed, "When you start thinking about . . . the inner mystery, inner life, the eternal life, there aren't too many images for you to use. You begin on your own, to have the images that are already present in some other system of thought."[20] "One explanation," says Campbell, "is that the human psyche is essentially the same all over the world. . . . Out of this common ground have come what Jung has called the archetypes, which are the common ideas of myths."[21]

Willis' paintings are extremely evocative and poetic, saturated with reference and meaning. They can take a long time to unravel, unfold, and reveal themselves. His paintings do not spell out their meanings in obvious ways. Indeed, his intention is not to make easy paintings, but to express an intangible feeling that is both universal and intensely personal. Verging on abstraction, his paintings are not always accessible. They are meant to be difficult in a sense, not wanting to give up meaning easily, insisting instead for some effort on the viewer's part.

Willis, a voracious reader, has been influenced by Kakuzo Okakura's *The Book of Tea*, which was first published in 1906 and uses the tea ceremony as a metaphor for Japanese culture and tradition. References to Okakura in Willis' recent work can be seen most literally in *Tea Vessel* (1988, cat. 20), a small, vibrant green, black, and brown painting. About art, Okakura writes, "In leaving something unsaid the beholder is given a chance to complete the idea and thus a great masterpiece irresistibly rivets your attention until you seem to become actually a part of it. A vacuum is there for you to enter and fill up to the full measure of your aesthetic emotion."[22] The power of Willis' art lies in suggesting instead of exposing. "Teaism," wrote Okakura, "is the art of concealing beauty that you may discover it, of suggesting what you dare not reveal."[23]

It is not surprising that the subtle colors and nuances in paintings like Willis' are difficult to perceive. Accustomed to immediacy in an age of FAX machines, car phones, microwaves, computers, and video, we expect gratification quickly and effortlessly. Willis' works remind us that some things are best revealed in their own time. His paintings are objects for contemplation, transcendent and sublime, rareties in our fast-moving world. They are works that one can get lost in, a total immersion that can cause one to forget about the external world. Dense, concentrated, and powerful, his enduring images imprint themselves in one's subconscious.

Born and raised in the southern countryside—the small towns, swamps, and woods of rural Alabama, Georgia, and Florida—Willis has returned to nature and a rural lifestyle as a place of solitude and refuge and as a source of inspiration. Deliberately choosing to work outside of the mainstream, Willis lives in a small town (Preston, Maryland, population 500) on the Eastern Shore of the Chesapeake Bay, near the Choptank River. He commutes to Washington, D.C., several times a week to teach and frequently goes to New York, but he finds that he works better outside the city, where he can have a simple lifestyle and a closeness to nature that is rooted in his childhood.

In his conscious choice to live in a rural area, Willis resembles the American Transcendentalist writers, Henry David Thoreau, Ralph Waldo Emerson, and Walt Whitman, and the American modernist artists such as Arthur Dove, Georgia O'Keeffe, and Charles Burchfield, all of whom sought refuge and inspiration in nature. In fact, Willis cites a painting by Burchfield—*Night of the Equinox* (ca.

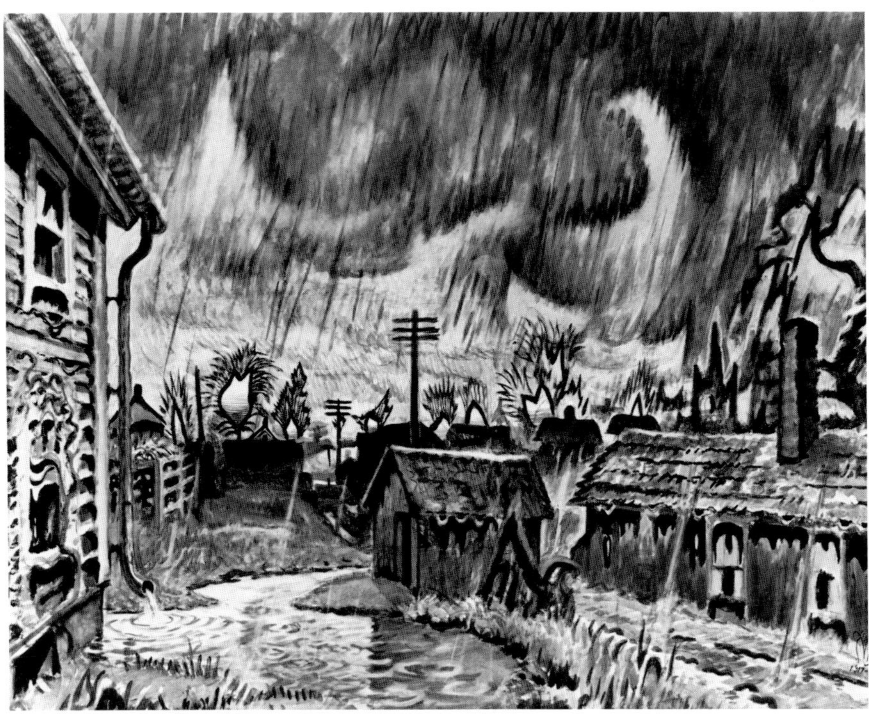

Fig. 6. Charles Burchfield, *Night of the Equinox*, ca. 1917-55, watercolor, brush, and charcoal on paper, 40 x 52. National Museum of American Art, Smithsonian Institution. Gift of the Sara Roby Foundation

Fig. 7. Arthur Dove, *Cows in Pasture*, 1935, wax emulsion on canvas, 20 x 28. The Phillips Collection, Washington, D.C.

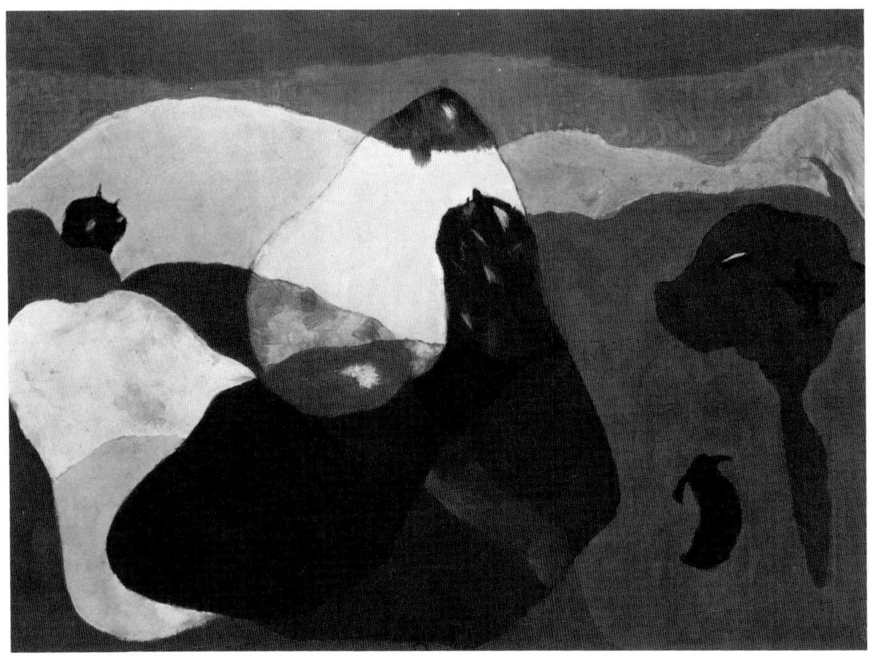

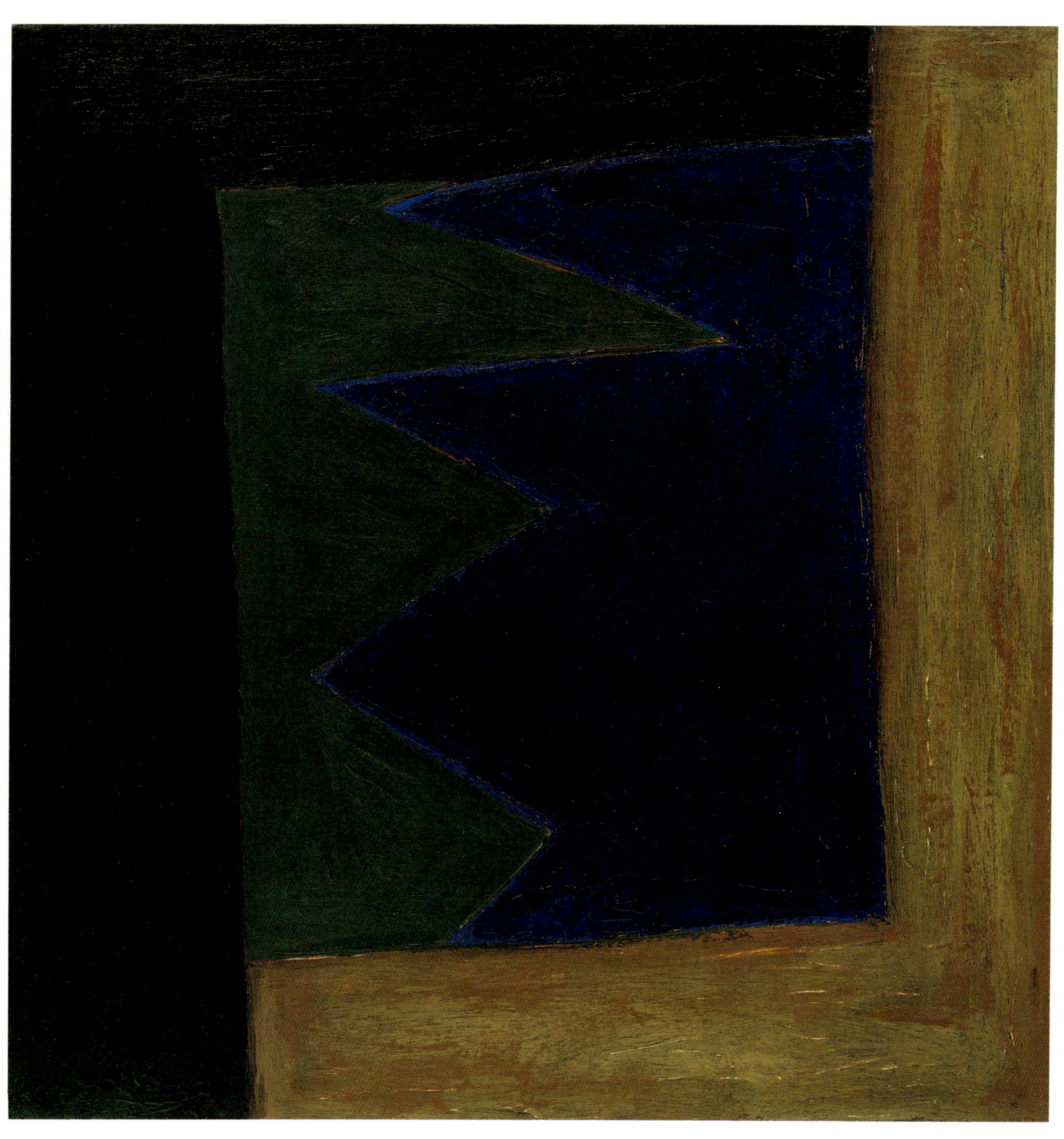

Cat. 11. *Edge of Influence*, 1978-85, oil on canvas, 22 x 22. Private Collection

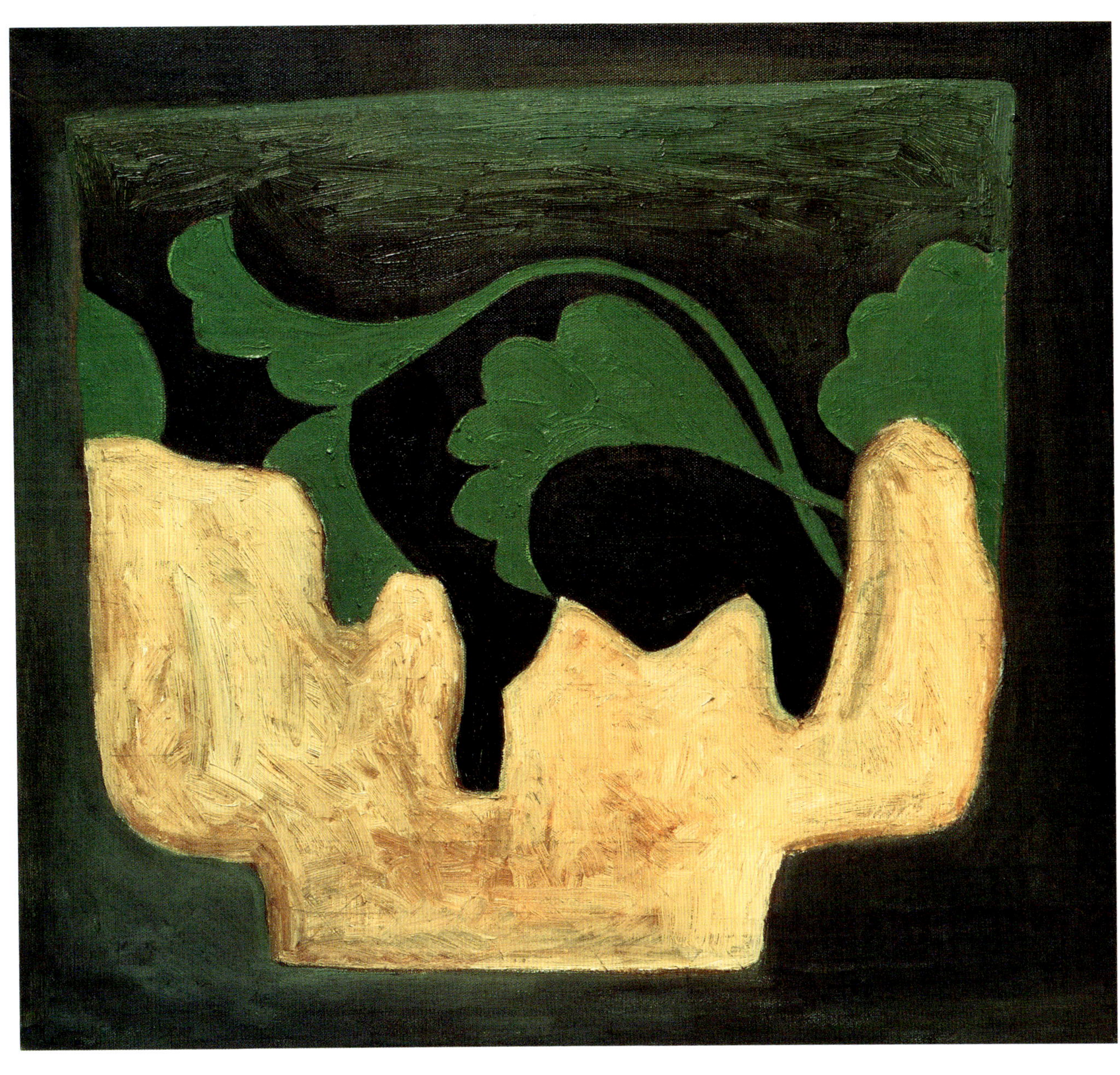

Cat. 20. *Tea Vessel*, 1988, oil on canvas, 18 x 20. Private Collection

1917–55, fig. 6)—as having affected his decision to become an artist instead of an engineer. Similarities can be seen between Willis' work and the paintings of these early twentieth-century artists, who simplified and abstracted natural forms to materialize the essence of things and places, suggesting something beyond the physical world, as in Arthur Dove's *Cows in Pasture* (1935, fig. 7). To the American modernists, the landscape stood for something deeper than its literal depiction; the forms of nature became visual equivalents for personal visions and experiences.[24]

Willis does not paint directly from the observed landscape, but he is inspired by nature, and his restrained palette consists of the muted colors and tones of his rural environment. These colors can be seen in works such as *Untitled (Ledger)* (1988, cat. 25), with its luminescent greens, velvet blacks, matte grays, and earth browns, with some areas thickly painted and others scraped away. In describing his choice of colors, Willis has said, "If I want to look for examples of color to learn from or inspire me, I go to nature. And that's where I think I get accused of using 'muddy' colors. I see the beauty inherent in the earth banks of a river bed. I love it out on the Eastern Shore because of the somberness of the grays and the dead blackish greens—to me it is just so beautiful. Then when you do see something bright, like the bright red on the wing of a red-winged blackbird, when nature uses a bright color, it's so effective. It's used with just the right amount, the right accent, the right proportion—I guess that's the way I try to approach it."[25]

Wary of the sensuous quality of bright colors, Willis rarely uses them. He finds that they are often too seductive, too dominant in a painting. When he does use a vibrant color the impact is powerful, as in *The Persistent Fool* (1981, cat. 4), the title of which comes from a passage by William Blake: "Even a fool if he persists in his folly will become wise." The colors in this painting are primarily subdued and muted—the blacks, browns, and greens of a murky swamp—but it is also punctuated by stark white and vibrant green shapes and a small but intense diamond-shaped area of bright red that focuses everything on the center of the painting and almost jumps out of the canvas, like the tongue of a snake about to strike. In the ambiguous background, glimpses of residual images can be seen through the many layers of paint, but the vividly colored shapes that cut into it are clearly delineated. Playing shiny against matte, bright against dark, vertical against horizontal, a tension is created by these opposing forces. Completely covering the canvas, this painting commands an incredible presence in a room, consuming the space around it.

Instead of working with the stimulating, immediate, pure tones of primary colors, Willis is more interested in exploring the gradations in tone and value of more subtle colors. The one exception to this restrained palette, the one "seductive" color that does consistently appear in his work, is blue. In *Untitled (Blue Screen)* (1988, cat. 22) and *Lotus Pond I* (1989, cat. 26), the content lies in the color more than in the image. These are extremely beautiful, serene, seductive, evocative paintings. *Untitled (Blue Screen)* is composed of undulating plantlike forms and circular patterns that bring to mind the ripples on the surface of a pond. The blue, and the forms it takes in many of Willis' paintings, alludes to water, which in Hindu mythology "represents the element of the deeper unconscious" and "has been regarded in India as a tangible manifestation of the divine essence."[26]

In the painting *The Path to Blue* (1981, cat. 5), the blue does not completely cover the field of the canvas as it does in *Untitled (Blue Screen)*, but it does become the focal point. When he painted this work in 1981, Willis

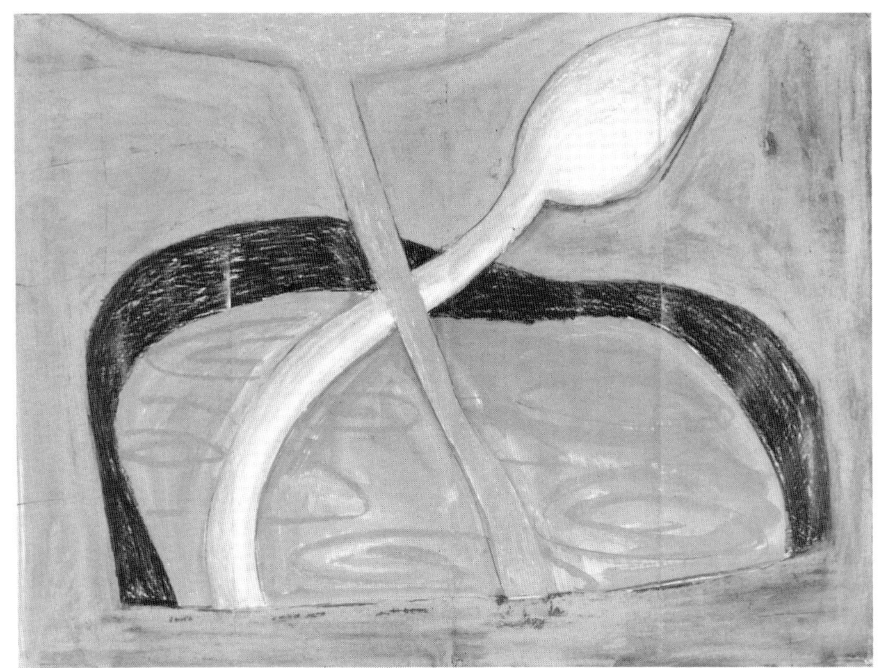

Cat. 26. *Lotus Pond I*, 1989, pencil, pastel, oil crayon, and watercolor on paper, 18 x 24. Courtesy of Baumgartner Galleries, Washington, D.C., and Rosa Esman Gallery, New York

was immersed in yoga and the teachings of Muktananda, and the blue alludes to the "blue light experience," the phenomenon of seeing a blue light while meditating. Blue becomes a symbol for enlightenment, the light that one will reach at the end of the path to devotion. The blue in *The Path to Blue* is intense, electric, vibrant, generating and radiating light and energy. As in most of Willis' work, the light comes from within the painting, rather than from an outside source. He tends to paint at night, with artificial light rather than natural light, because he likes having light that he can control.

"In painting, as in life, completeness is essentially a process of removal, of carving away non-essentials, of eventually arriving at the source. This is what my work is about. I bow to that Source. Om Namah Shivaya." William Willis, *1986*[27]

Seemingly simple at first glance, closer observation reveals the complexity and the innumerable layers—of both paint and meaning—that make up Willis' paintings. Often extremely labored, his paintings are worked and reworked; images appear only to be painted over until they disappear. Willis often works on paintings over a span of years, such as *Edge of Influence* (1978–85, cat. 11), *Untitled (Kalaśa)* (1986–88, cat. 19), and *Screen with Lotus* (1978–88, cat. 18). He has painted over a painting that was once "finished" and exhibited, transforming it into something completely different. Willis applies and removes paint with trowels, scrapers, brushes, palette knives, ceramic tools, occasionally even using a power sander, turning painting into a process in which taking paint off is as important as putting it on. He cuts canvases in half and puts them back together again, notches corners, and incorporates cut-out forms and collaged elements from other works. Transforming a two-dimensional medium into a three-dimensional form, he emphasizes the physical quality of a painting, the painting as an object.

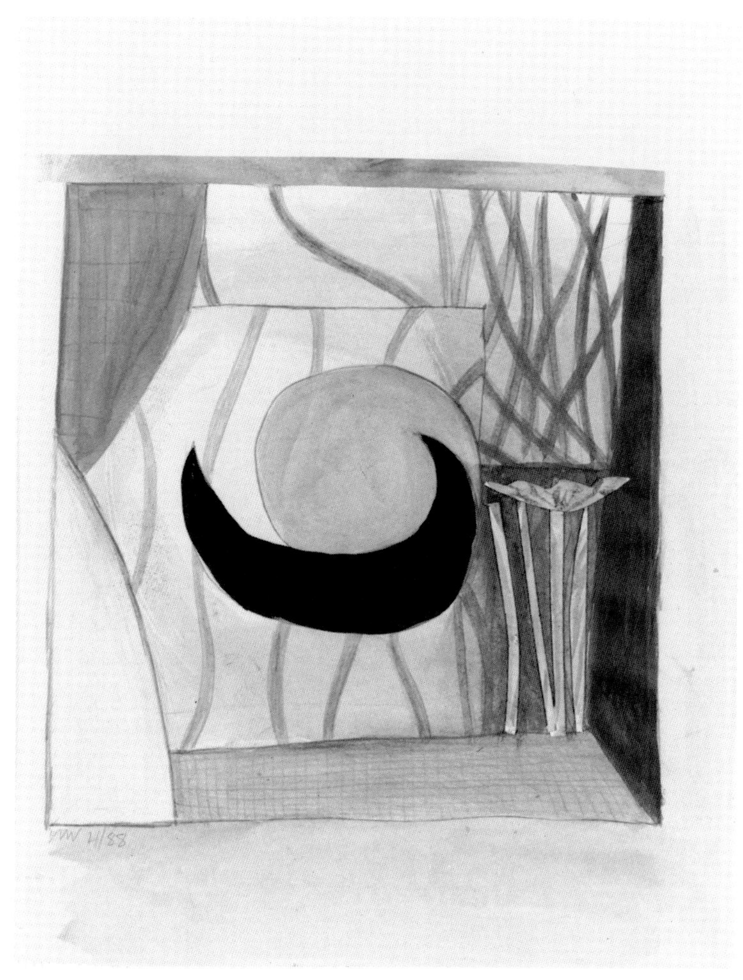

Cat. 24. *Untitled (Black Moon)*, 1988, pencil, gouache, and watercolor on paper, 13¾ x 10⅝. Courtesy of Baumgartner Galleries, Washington, D.C., and Rosa Esman Gallery, New York

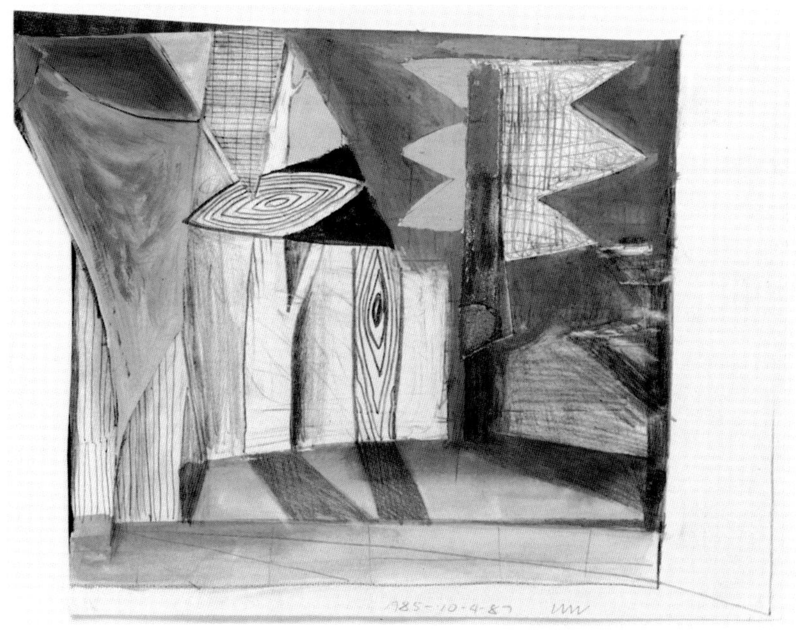

Cat. 15. *Trees in the Backyard*, 1985-87, pencil, ink, and gouache on paper, 9 x 12. Collection of the artist

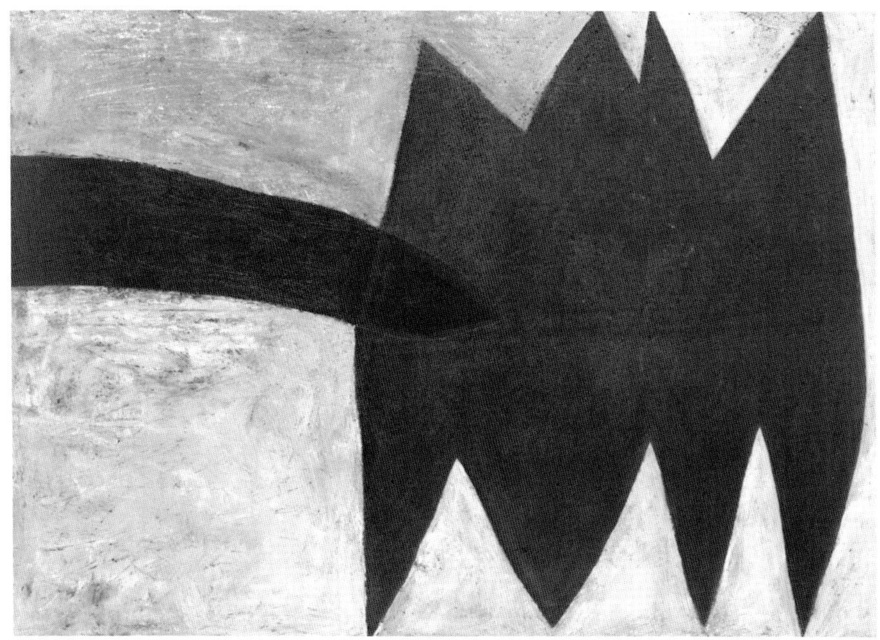

Cat. 7. *Falling Tree*, 1982, oil and dirt on canvas, 61¾ x 88½. Collection of the artist

As Willis recently described himself, "I think I am probably a sculptor working out my problems in paint."[28]

Willis works on several paintings at a time, going back and forth from one to another, from paper to canvas. Many of the works on paper combine mixed media—gouache, watercolor, pastel, chalk, charcoal, pencil, acrylic, oil—with collaged and cut-out sections taken from other drawings, as can be seen in *Untitled (Black Moon)* (1988, cat. 24) and *Trees in the Backyard* (1985–87, cat. 15). Many of the smaller works are pages removed from the notebooks in which he writes, sketches, and keeps notes on paintings as he works on them and changes them. The works on paper are rarely studies for the paintings; sometimes the drawings are used as a point of departure to get a painting started, but they are usually transformed into completely different images. *Tree* (1988, cat. 23) is a minimal but compelling work. A small, cut-out gray tree, it concentrates many of Willis' concerns into one powerful, evocative image—his love of grays, the symbolic zig-zag shape, his close connection to nature. *Tree* is extremely emblematic and iconic; nature abstracted and concentrated, it materializes the essence of a tree.

Falling Tree (1982, cat. 7) is a painting that Willis struggled to complete. It started out as a vertical tree, but at one point, frustrated with the direction that it was taking, feeling that it was "too precious," he put it on the floor and threw a handful of dirt on it. That action was enough of a catalyst to push it in the right direction, and he finished it. A few months later, he saw the painting lying on its side in his studio and decided to leave it that way, as a fallen tree. "Then several more months later, I was reading some philosophical stuff, and I found a [passage] that went something like this: Traveling through the forest of ignorance, I felled the trees, working towards [divine] knowledge."[29]

Through the layers of paint that are built up on the surfaces of Willis' paintings one can see the vestiges of earlier images that have been painted out. These residual shapes can be seen in *Untitled (Kalaśa)* (1986–88, cat. 19), the surface, color, and composition of which are reminiscent of the paintings of the contemporary British artist John Walker, whom Willis admires. Some areas are thickly painted and then scratched, scraped, and carved out, others are thinly painted and more transparent. Traces of a grid and the shadows of a zig-zag form can be glimpsed through the atmospheric layers of paint. The undulating white line on the vessel in the foreground jumps off the surface, pushing forward. The white line stands for shakti, the Hindu symbol of vibrating energy, and the vessel itself alludes to the Hindu symbolism of "a jar or pitcher—representing the presence of the divinity, standing in the place of a sacred image."[30]

Like Walker's paintings, such as *Untitled* (1977, fig. 8), the surfaces of Willis' canvases are extremely textured and tactile, emphasizing the

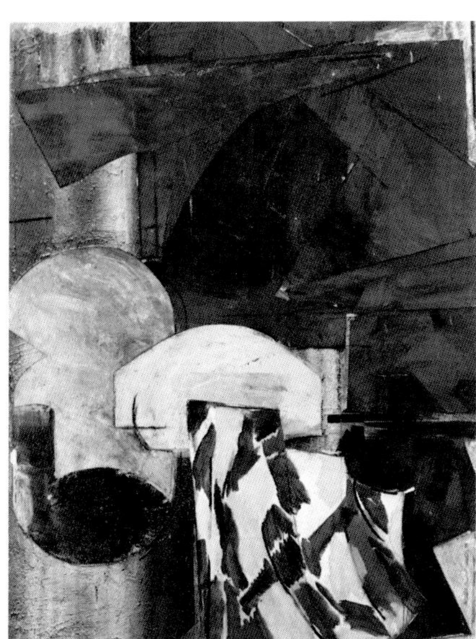

Fig. 8. John Walker, *Untitled*, 1977, acrylic, chalk, and canvas collage on canvas, 120 x 96. The Phillips Collection, Washington, D.C.

physical quality of the painting. This focus on the painting as an object, not an illusion, is especially noticeable in works such as *Untitled (Ledger)* (1988, cat. 25), which has a notched corner where a section of the canvas in the upper right corner has been cut out. This painting is composed of an open book and an organic plantlike form; its title refers to an accounting book, a balancing of debit and credit. The removal of the corner brings attention back to the painting as a physical object. Playing object against image, it sets up an opposition between the illusion of the painted image and the physical reality of the canvas. Willis' works fit Jack Flam's description of Walker's paintings as works that "offer themselves as what they are—as physical objects made of paint worked by hand, in which are embedded the record of innumerable gestures."[31]

Willis' paintings, like those of Walker, lie in between abstraction and representation. Flam goes on to describe Walker's paintings as containing "a disquieting mixture of recognizable and abstract elements. . . . The paradox and enigma expressed in these paintings is at root a cognitive one: they clearly represent things, yet it is impossible to say just what those things are—how mysteriously unnameable their subjects are—the images, the ambiguity of certain parts will just not yield to a single reading."[32] Many of Willis' works, such as *The Garden*, *The Stones*, *Untitled (Ledger)*, and *The Screen*, consist of forms and images that verge on abstraction and yet are simultaneously pulled into recognition as they dredge up memories and trigger associations. This quality can be seen in *The Stones* (1987, cat. 17), which alludes to ancient stone monoliths, the prehistoric, mysterious formations of Stonehenge and Carnac.

Several of Willis' paintings refer to works by other artists. His recent still lifes, such as *Heroes*, *Untitled (Flyby)*, and *Untitled (Kalaśa)*, allude to the

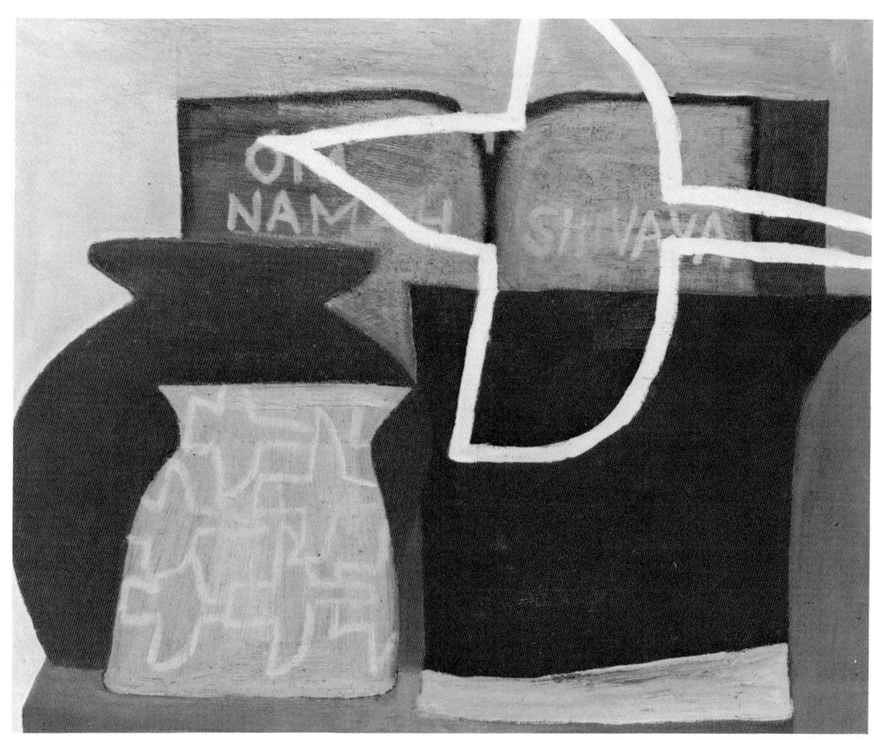

Cat. 27. *Untitled (Flyby)*, 1988-89, oil on canvas, 16 x 20. Collection of the artist

paintings of Morandi, Guston, and Braque (figs. 9, 10, 11). In Willis' still lifes, forms are pared down, details are reduced and every shape seems consciously selected for its part in the whole; nothing is extraneous. In contrast to earlier works, which completely covered the picture plane and seemed to expand beyond the edge of the canvas—such as *The Garden* (1985–87, cat. 14), *The Screen* (1983, cat. 9), and *Falling Tree* (1982, cat. 7)—these paintings from 1988–89 are more tightly composed. Moving away from the edge and into the center of the canvas, their clustered compositions push forms together into an interlocking, overlapping mass of flat, simplified, and concentrated shapes.

Heroes (1988, cat. 21), whose title refers to artists that Willis strongly admires—Guston, Morandi, Braque—translates Guston's figurative imagery, as can be seen in *The Lesson* (1975, fig. 9), into a still life composition in which a depiction of lifeless forms become an animated image. A simple still life is loaded with reference and association, infused with meaning. As in Braque's still lifes, such as *Pitcher, Pipe and Pear* (ca. 1924, fig. 10), the tabletop and objects in *Heroes* are pushed forward, compressing the already shallow space between surface and depth, flattening the forms, and tilting the picture plane into the viewer's space. Similarities can also be seen between the still lifes of *Heroes* and *Untitled (Flyby)* and Morandi's still lifes, such as *Still Life* (1950, fig. 11), with their clustered arrangements of bottles and vases and neutral backgrounds. Like Morandi, Willis creates evocative still lifes in which depictions of ordinary objects are imbued with a sense of something beyond the physical image of an arrangement of objects. In these works, Willis employs a subtle palette of earth tones that reflects his interest in and admiration of Morandi's use of color—muted, subdued, almost monochromatic, focusing on slight variations in tone and value in white, brown, and gray.

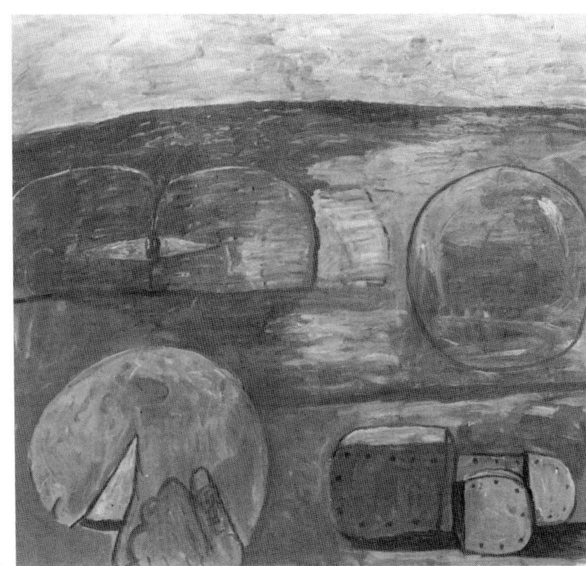

Fig. 9. Philip Guston, *The Lesson*, 1975, oil on canvas, 67$\frac{1}{4}$ x 72$\frac{1}{2}$. The Phillips Collection, Washington, D.C.

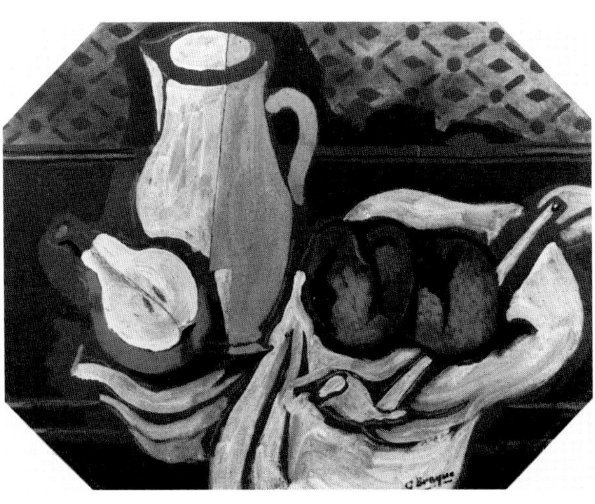

Fig. 10. Georges Braque, *Pitcher, Pipe and Pear*, ca. 1924, oil on wood panel, 13$\frac{3}{8}$ x 16$\frac{7}{8}$. The Phillips Collection, Washington, D.C.

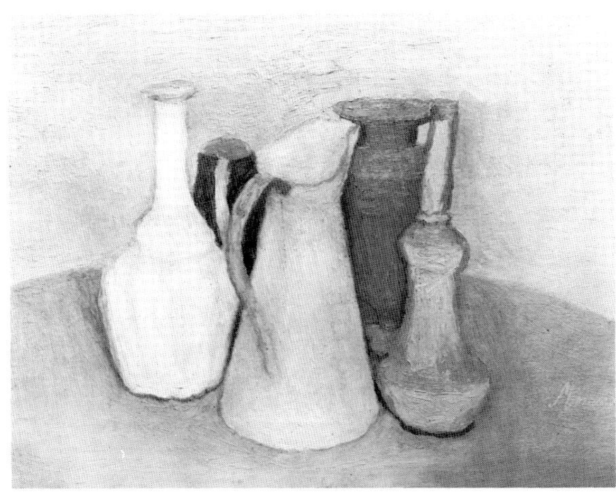

Fig. 11. Giorgio Morandi, *Still Life*, 1950, oil on canvas, 14$\frac{1}{8}$ x 18$\frac{5}{8}$. The Phillips Collection, Washington, D.C.

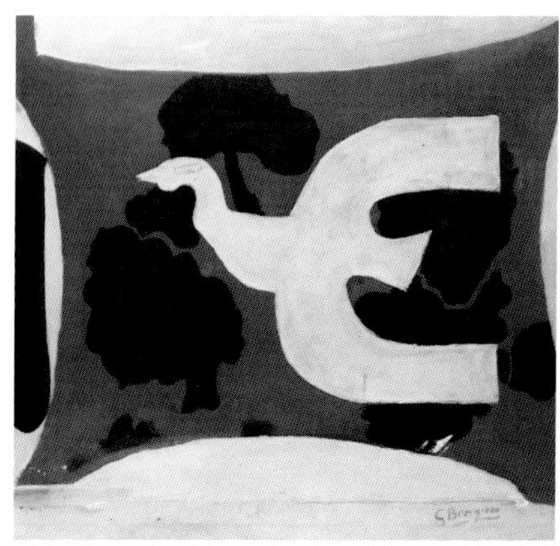

Fig. 12. Georges Braque, *Bird*, 1956, oil on canvas, 18 x 19½. The Phillips Collection, Washington, D.C.

These recent still lifes, not painted from actual, observed arrangements of objects, are symbolic paintings. The most recent, *Untitled (Flyby)* (1988–89, cat. 27), combines the image of an open book, inscribed with a mantra, with a group of vessels and the outline of a bird that appears to be flying by the tableau. Its head has already moved beyond the picture, out of our sight. Similar to the abstracted form of a bird that appears in many of Braque's works (fig. 12), Willis' silhouettes of birds, in works such as *Untitled (Flyby)* and *Haṁ Sa (The Gander)* (1989, cat. 28), hover between abstraction and representation. Like Braque's birds, Willis' birds float, suspended in flight, often isolated on the field of the canvas. In *Untitled (Flyby),* the bird appears both as a decorative pattern that covers the surface of a vase in the background and as an open shape in the foreground that cuts through the painting.

"I've always worked in cycles in my work where things are busy and complex and I pare them down to the essential, final ingredient—loving process, somehow letting the process dictate images and ideas."[33] For Willis, the process of creation is critical to the meaning of the painting, and at a certain point the process takes over. As he describes it, "You become the tool and the painting pulls you along."[34] Willis' view of the artist as a conduit for a universal source of creative energy reflects the traditional or primitive arts, which are usually anonymous creations because the artist is viewed as the "instrument" for something greater, and "art is only the means to an end."[35] The painting is the vehicle for something beyond the physical world, and during its creation the artist gives up control and surrenders to the process. Willis has discovered that his paintings will not work when he starts out trying to make them simple, that he cannot artificially create an image that is born out of process. As he says, "I realize that I just have to somehow make things more busy and more complex and then go about the activity of carving out the unessentials, and then all of a sudden I discover what works in terms of what's primary. . . . To me that's what's beauti-

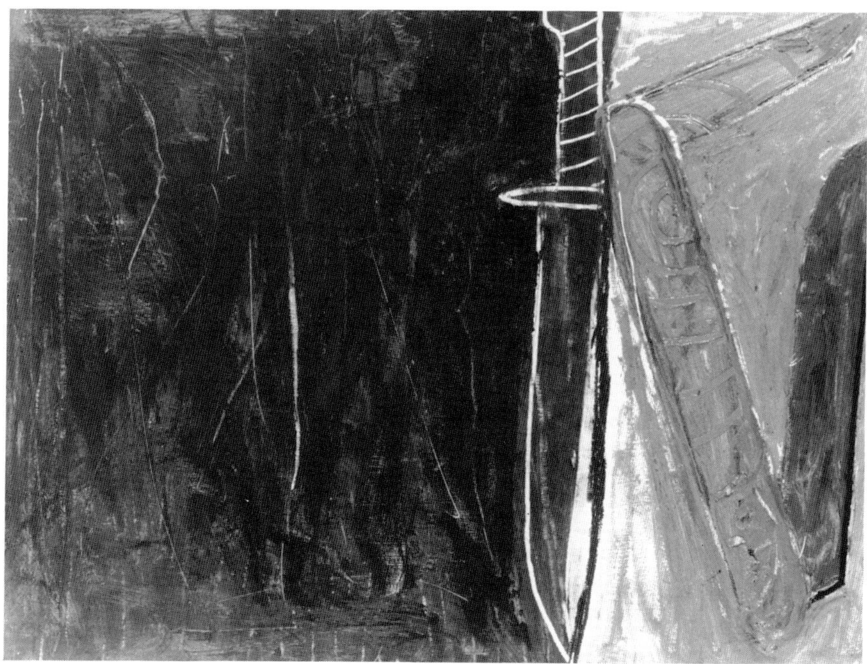

Cat. 6. *The Knife Myth*, 1982, oil on paper, 22 x 30. Collection of Murray Bring, New York

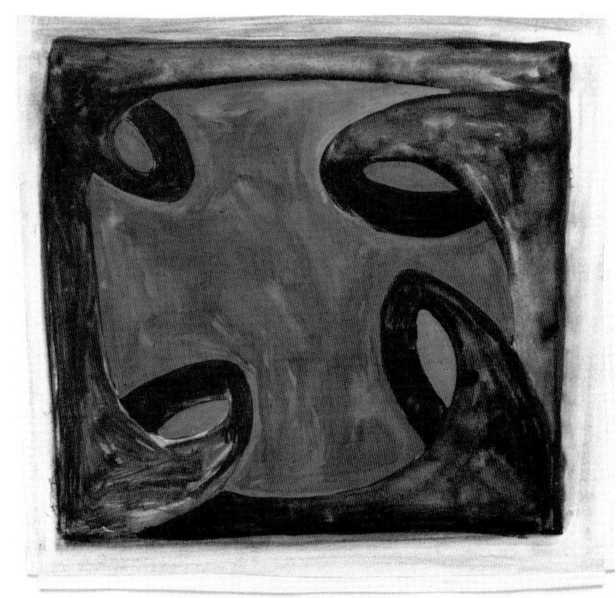

Cat. 12. *Untitled (Study for Kundalini Screen)*, 1985, gouache, watercolor, and pencil on paper, 10¼ x 9½. Collection of the artist

Cat. 17. *The Stones*, 1987, oil on canvas, 28 x 22. Collection of Manfred Baumgartner

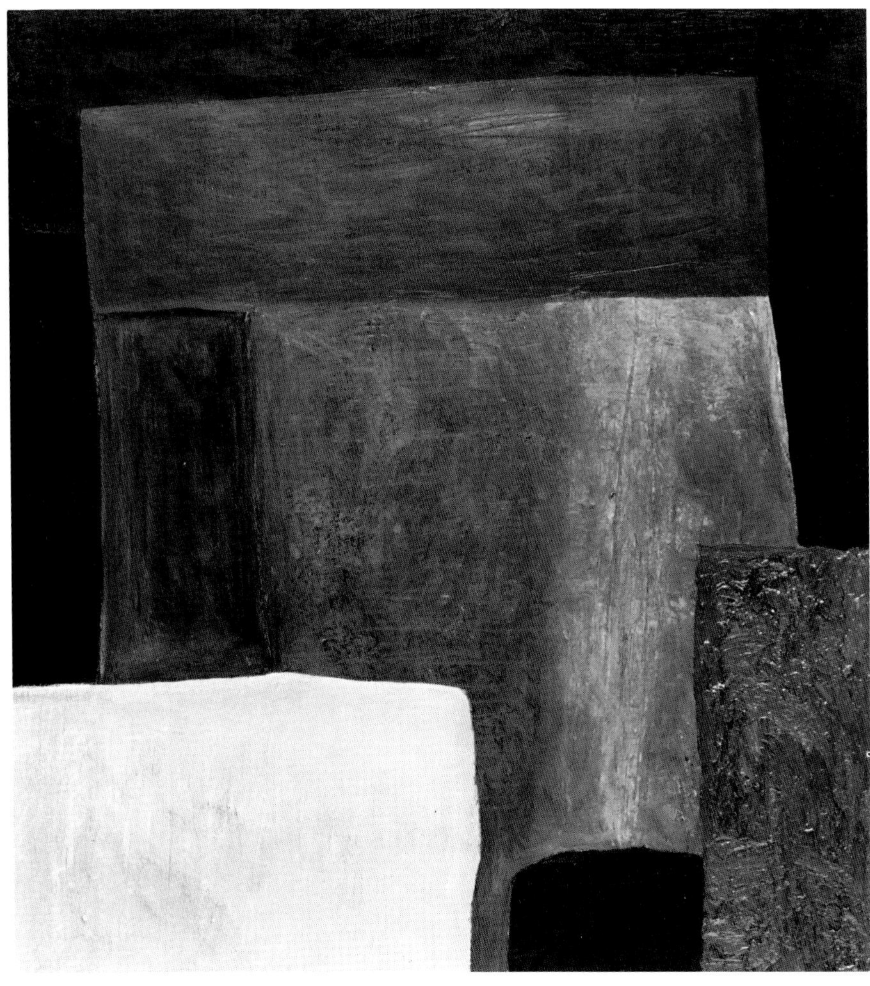

ful about the process; it works in a way that you think you've got the answer, but of course you don't.''[36]

''Certain artists do something and a new emotion is brought into the world; its real meaning lies outside of history and chains of causality. . . . Human consciousness moves, but it is not a leap: it is one inch. One inch is a small jump, but that jump is everything.''

Philip Guston[37]

We live in a world where we have severed our connections to myth and symbolism, lost our rituals to live by, and removed the mystery from our lives. Reinfusing art with myth, ritual, symbolism, and mystery, the archetypal images of Willis' evocative and elusive paintings return us to our primal roots, to the universal, transtheological sources of life and creativity that give meaning to our lives.

In *The Power of Myth*, Joseph Camp-

Cat. 23. *Tree*, 1988, mixed media on paper, 7¼ x 3¼. Collection of the artist

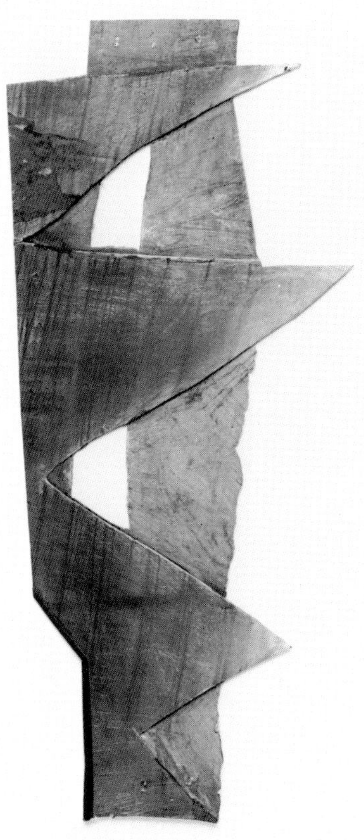

Cat. 8. *Trees of Ignorance*, 1982, oil and charcoal on paper, 30 x 34. Collection of Peter Carley, Washington, D.C.

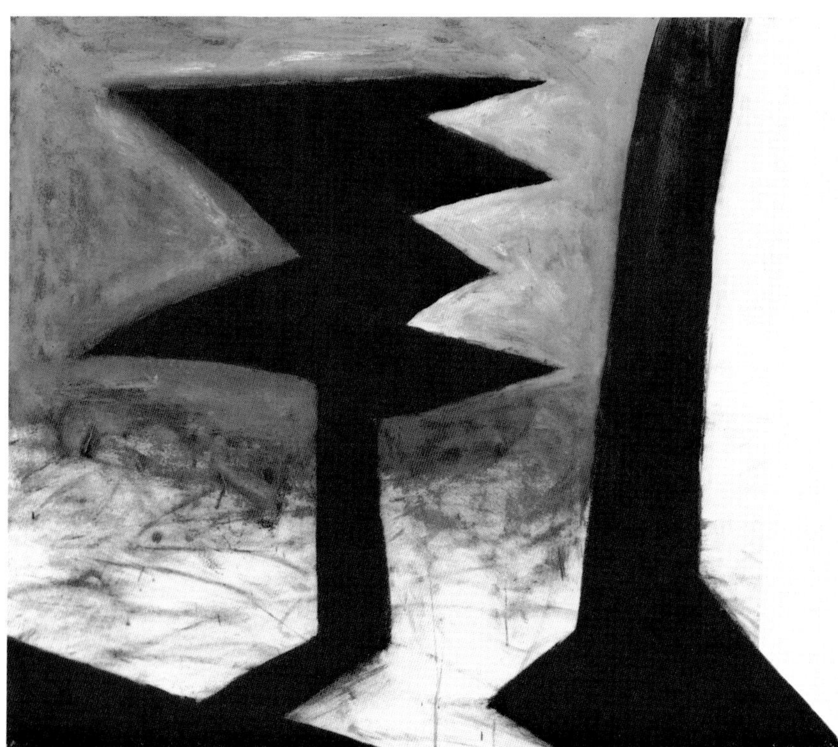

bell discusses the similarities between the myths and symbols of different cultures. These stories of creation, destruction, resurrection, and rites of passage appear throughout time and across continents with slight variations, but the themes are basically the same. Choosing images that have the potential to move one beyond the physical plane, transcending the material world, Willis incorporates the elements that speak to him from these various myths and religions. *Screen with Lotus* (1978–88, cat. 18) is a complex work on paper that Willis has worked and reworked over the past decade. It melds many of his sources and influences into one intricate image, combining several of his symbols—the lotus, the screen, the undulating patterns of rippling water, the colors found in nature—into detailed layers of pattern, form, and meaning. In his work, Willis amalgamates and transforms the symbols and metaphors that best express the underlying source of all things, the source Campbell has described as "an undefinable, inconceivable mystery, thought of as a power, that is the source and end and supporting ground for all life and being."[38]

Willis does not tie himself to a specific religion or particular belief system. He is not seeking "spirituality" or "enlightenment," but he is looking for a completeness, a balance in his life and his work between the physical and spiritual, the conscious and unconscious, the intellectual and the intuitive. As Willis has described it, it is only when art can combine these polar opposites, when it "somehow fuses [these polarities] together and has a life of its own that it is interesting."[39] William Willis' paintings speak to our bodies and souls, hearts and minds, in an evocative, poetic, visual language, born out of universal and personal symbols, myths, references, and memories, eluding specific definitions and set limitations, existing in a space between moment and memory.

Notes

1. Quoted in Joseph Campbell, with Bill Moyers, *The Power of Myth*, ed. Betty Sue Flowers (New York: Doubleday, 1988), 55.

2. Philip Guston, quoted in Robert Storr, *Philip Guston* (New York: Abbeville Press, 1986), 22.

3. Conversation with the artist, April 5, 1989.

4. Heinrich Zimmer, *Myths and Symbols in Indian Art and Civilization*, ed. Joseph Campbell (New York: Harper and Row, 1946), 40, 41.

5. Kakuzo Okakura, *The Book of Tea* (1906; reprint, New York: Dover Publications, 1964), 45.

6. Guston, quoted in Storr, 28.

7. Lecture by the artist at the Corcoran Gallery of Art, Washington, D.C., March 24, 1988.

8. Conversation with the artist, April 5, 1989.

9. Ibid.

10. William Willis, quoted in an interview with Mary Swift, *Washington Review*, April/May 1988, 19. Annotated by Willis, August 3, 1989.

11. For translations and discussions of Eastern mythology and symbolism, see Zimmer, *Myths and Symbols in Indian Art and Civilization*, and Ananda K. Coomaraswamy, *Christian and Oriental Philosophy of Art* (New York: Dover Publications, 1956).

12. Douglas McCreary Greenwood, "The Mantra and Yantra of William Willis," *Dossier*, March 1988, 79.

13. Campbell, 56, 57.

14. Conversation with the artist, April 5, 1989.

15. Willis, quoted in Swift, *Washington Review*, 20.

16. Zimmer, 25.

17. Ibid., 49–50.

18. Ibid., 48.

19. Swami Muktananda, *Kundalini: The Secret of Life* (South Fallsburg, N.Y.: SYDA Foundation, 1979), 14.

20. Campbell, 39.

21. Ibid., 51.

22. Okakura, 24, 25.

23. Ibid., 7.

24. Linda L. Johnson, *American Modernism* (Washington, D.C.: The Phillips Collection, 1989), unpaginated.

25. Conversation with the artist, April 5, 1989.

26. Zimmer, 45, 34.

27. Willis, quoted in *Awards in the Visual Arts* (Winston-Salem, N.C.: Southeastern Center for Contemporary Art, 1987), 110.

28. Willis started out studying sculpture and eventually ended up as a painter, although for a while the two merged when in the early 1970s, influenced by Jasper Johns and Robert Rauschenberg, he incorporated found objects in his paintings. Conversation with the artist, April 5, 1989.

29. Willis, quoted in Jane Addams Allen, "Corcoran Selects Willis for 'Spectrum,'" *Washington Times*, October 15, 1988, E5. Annotated by Willis, August 3, 1989.

30. Zimmer, 34.

31. Jack Flam, *John Walker* (Washington, D.C.: The Phillips Collection, 1982), unpaginated.

32. Ibid.

33. Conversation with the artist, April 5, 1989.

34. Ibid.

35. Coomaraswamy, 52–53.

36. Conversation with the artist, April 5, 1989.

37. Guston, quoted in Storr, 99.

38. Campbell, 31.

39. Conversation with the artist, April 5, 1989.

Chronology

1943 Born January 31 in Sheffield, Alabama. Grows up in Alabama, Georgia, and Florida.

1961–68 Enters University of South Florida, Tampa, to study engineering. Sees Charles Burchfield's painting, *Night of the Equinox,* in Sarah Roby Foundation exhibition at the university art gallery. Eventually changes major to art, studying painting and sculpture. Receives B.A. in 1968.

1967 Marries Ann (Mimi) Falkner.

1968 Birth of son, William Dewey III.

1969 Graduates from U.S. Naval Reserve Officer Training School, Newport, Rhode Island.

Birth of son, Michael Seth.

1969–71 Serves active duty in the U.S. Naval Reserve.

1971–73 Studies painting at University of South Florida, Tampa. Receives M.F.A. in 1973.

1974–83 Moves to Adelphi, Maryland. Accepts teaching position at the University of Maryland, College Park. Continues teaching painting, drawing, and printmaking until 1983.

1977 Sees Horace Pippin exhibition at The Phillips Collection, Washington, D.C.

First solo exhibition at Diane Brown Gallery, Washington, D.C.

1979 Becomes involved with Siddha Yoga after visiting a meditation center with friend, Joe Ferrioli.

1980 Meets Swami Muktananda at ashram in the Catskills, New York. Continues to visit ashram every summer.

Moves to Preston, Maryland.

Receives grant from the National Endowment for the Arts.

1981 First solo exhibition in New York at Bernard Jacobson Gallery.

1982 Sees exhibition, "Georges Braque: The Late Paintings," at The Phillips Collection.

1985 Starts teaching painting at the Corcoran School of Art, Washington, D.C., where he continues to teach up to the present.

Solo exhibition at the Washington Project for the Arts.

1986 First solo exhibition at Baumgartner Galleries, Washington, D.C.

1987 Receives Award in the Visual Arts from the Southeastern Center for Contemporary Art, Winston-Salem, N.C.; exhibition of award recipients travels to New York, Ohio, and California.

First solo exhibition at Rosa Esman Gallery, New York.

Receives Pollock-Krasner Foundation grant.

Public Collections

Artery Organization, Inc., Chevy Chase, Maryland
Best Products Company, Inc., Richmond, Virginia
Oliver T. Carr Company, Washington, D.C.
The Corcoran Gallery of Art, Washington, D.C.
U.S. Department of Health and Human Services, Washington, D.C.
U.S. Department of the Treasury, Washington, D.C.
Dickinson State College, Dickinson, North Dakota
Megatrends, Ltd., Washington, D.C.
Minot State College, Minot, North Dakota
Peat Marwick Main and Company, Washington, D.C.
Philip Morris Companies, Inc., New York
The Phillips Collection, Washington, D.C.
Prudential Insurance Company of America, Newark, New Jersey
University of Maryland, College Park
University of South Florida, Tampa
Vesti Corporation, Boston, Massachusetts

Exhibition History

Selected Individual Exhibitions

1977 Diane Brown Gallery, Washington, D.C.

1979 Diane Brown Gallery, Washington, D.C.

1981 Bernard Jacobson Gallery, New York
Jack Rasmussen Gallery, Washington, D.C.

1982 I. Irving Feldman Gallery, Southfield, Michigan

1985 Washington Project for the Arts, Washington, D.C.

1986 Baumgartner Galleries, Washington, D.C.

1987 Baumgartner Galleries, Washington, D.C.
Grand Rapids Art Museum, Grand Rapids, Michigan
Rosa Esman Gallery, New York

1988 Reynolds/Minor Gallery, Richmond, Virginia

Selected Group Exhibitions

1976 "Washington Painters," Art Gallery, Rutgers University, Camden, New Jersey

1978 "Maryland Biennial," Baltimore Museum of Art, Baltimore, Maryland

1979 "On and Of Paper," De Land Museum of Art, De Land, Florida

"Elements of Art: Texture," Arlington Arts Center, Arlington, Virginia

1980 "Maryland Invitational," The Arts Gallery, Baltimore, Maryland

1981 "Black and White Drawings," Jack Rasmussen Gallery, Washington, D.C.

1982 "Artscape," Decker & Meyerhoff Galleries, Maryland Institute, College of Art, Baltimore, Maryland

1983 "Biennial Exhibition," Baltimore Museum of Art, Baltimore, Maryland

"Maryland Collects," Maryland Art Place, Baltimore, Maryland

1984 Washington Project for the Arts, Washington, D.C.

1985 "Evocative Abstraction," NEXUS/The Foundation for Today's Art, Philadelphia, Pennsylvania

"Exchange: Drawings of American and Indian Artists," Art Heritage Gallery, Triveni Kala Sangam, New Delhi, India (traveled: Bombay, Calcutta, Madras)

"Talent," Baumgartner Galleries, Washington, D.C.

"Tradition and Innovation," Dimock Gallery, George Washington University, Washington, D.C.

"The Washington Show," Corcoran Gallery of Art, Washington, D.C.

1986 "10 Washington, D.C., Painters," Southeastern Center for Contemporary Art, Winston-Salem, North Carolina

"Ten Artists Working in New York City and Washington, D.C.," Addison Gallery of American Art, Phillips Academy, Andover, Massachusetts

1987 "Awards in the Visual Arts 6," organized by Southeastern Center for Contemporary Art, Winston-Salem, North Carolina (traveled: Grey Art Gallery and Study Center, New York University, New York; Contemporary Arts Center, Cincinnati, Ohio; Newport Harbor Art Museum, Newport Beach, California)

"Invitational: Looking at New Work," Rosa Esman Gallery, New York

1988 "Natural Selection: Six Abstract Painters From Washington, D.C.," Spaces, Cleveland, Ohio

"Recollections: Washington Artists at WPA, 1975–88," Washington Project for the Arts, Washington, D.C.

"Significant Movement: Evocative Painting," Anton Gallery, Washington, D.C.

"Spectrum: Clifford Ross and William Willis," Corcoran Gallery of Art, Washington, D.C.

"Transcendence: Washington, D.C.," Baumgartner Galleries, Washington, D.C.

Selected Bibliography

Forgey, Benjamin. "Ironies and Memories in a Painter's Cantos." *Washington Star-News*, October 14, 1979, D3.

Lewis, Jo Ann. "Galleries." *Washington Post*, October 20, 1979, F7.

Mahoney, J.W. "East Coast Reviews: William Willis." *New Art Examiner*, December 1981, 16.

Harris, R.P. "M.A.P. Exhibit Reveals the Art of Ownership." *Baltimore Sun*, April 16, 1983, B1, B3.

Blumenthal, Diane. "East Coast Reviews." *New Art Examiner*, June 1984, 16.

Fleming, Lee. "Art Reviews." *Washington Review*, June/July 1984, 25.

Richard, Paul. "Galleries." *Washington Post*, April 21, 1984, B2.

Allen, Jane Addams. "Galleries: Intensity of Myths, Movement of Life." *Washington Times*, March 8, 1985, B3.

Coleman, Nicols. "Washington, D.C., Reviews." *New Art Examiner*, March 1985, 60.

Forgey, Benjamin. "Galleries: Big and Strong." *Washington Post*, February 16, 1985, C2.

Frank, Patrick. "Washington, D.C., Reviews." *New Art Examiner*, April 1985, 62.

Lewis, Jo Ann. "William Willis' Abstractions." *Washington Post*, April 19, 1986, D2.

Welzenbach, Michael. "Enduring Images—Sizable and Simple." *Washington Times*, April 10, 1986, 3B.

Bell, Tiffany. "Awards in the Visual Arts 6." *Art News*, September 1987, 139.

Forgey, Benjamin. "William Willis at Baumgartner." *Washington Post*, October 31, 1987, D2.

Krissoff, Sylvia. "Avant Garde: Symbolism and Color Are The Focal Points in William Willis Paintings." *Grand Rapids Press*, February 15, 1987, J8.

Rubenfeld, Florence. "William Willis: Works on Paper." *Museum & Arts Washington*, November/December 1987, 25.

Schwabsky, Barry. "The Persistence of American Art," *Awards in the Visual Arts 6* (exhibition catalogue). Winston-Salem, N.C.: Southeastern Center for Contemporary Art, 1987.

Thorson, Alice. "Late Blooming Willis, A Stylist of Simple Form." *Washington Times*, October 15, 1987, E3.

Allen, Jane Addams. "Corcoran Selects Willis for 'Spectrum.'" *Washington Times*, January 20, 1988, E1, E5.

Beardsley, John. *Spectrum: Clifford Ross and William Willis* (exhibition brochure). Washington, D.C.: Corcoran Gallery of Art, 1988.

Cohrs, Timothy. "Reviews: William Willis." *Art News*, January 1988, 163–64.

Greenwood, Douglas McCreary. "The Mantra and Yantra of William Willis." *Dossier*, March 1988, 36, 79.

Kolmer, Pat. "William Willis, Works on Paper." *Washington Review*, February/March 1988, 20.

Mahoney, J.W. "Review of Exhibitions: 'Transcendence' at Baumgartner." *Art in America*, April 1988, 213–14.

McCoy, Mary. "Art Reviews: Spectrum: Clifford Ross and William Willis." *Washington Review*, April/May 1988, 24–25.

Merritt, Robert. "Simple Forms Transcend Literal Interpretation." *Richmond Times-Dispatch*, October 1, 1988, A-12.

Reynolds, Jock. *Recollections: Washington Artists at WPA, 1975–88* (exhibition catalogue). Washington, D.C.: Washington Project for the Arts, 1988.

Richard, Paul. "The Search for Abstract Meaning." *Washington Post*, January 21, 1988, B1, B2.

Risatti, Howard. "Reviews: Transcendence: Washington, D.C." *Artforum*, April 1988, 152.

Rubenfeld, Florence. "Transcendence and the Centered Self." *New Art Examiner*, April 1988, 28–30.

Swift, Mary. "William Willis" (interview). *Washington Review*, April/May 1988, 19–22.

Catalogue of the Exhibition

Dimensions are given in inches, followed by centimeters, with height preceding width.

1. *Hyena*, 1977
oil on gessoed paper
50½ x 44¼ (128.3 x 112.4)
The Phillips Collection, Washington, D.C.
Gift of Mr. John Naisbitt and Ms. Patricia Aburdene, 1989

2. *Rain Storm for Horace Pippin*, 1979
oil on canvas
63¼ x 80 (160.7 x 203.2)
Best Products Company, Inc., Richmond, Virginia

3. *Flaming House*, 1981
dirt and charcoal on paper
26 x 41 (66.0 x 104.1)
Collection of Sherry Jones and Alan Stone, Washington, D.C.

4. *The Persistent Fool*, 1981
oil on canvas
90 x 108 (228.6 x 274.3)
Courtesy of Baumgartner Galleries, Washington, D.C., and Rosa Esman Gallery, New York

5. *The Path to Blue*, 1981
oil on canvas
67 x 89 (170.2 x 226.1)
Collection of John Deardourff and Elisabeth Griffith

6. *The Knife Myth*, 1982
oil on paper
22 x 30 (55.9 x 76.2)
Collection of Murray Bring, New York

7. *Falling Tree*, 1982
oil and dirt on canvas
61¾ x 88½ (156.9 x 224.8)
Collection of the artist

8. *Trees of Ignorance*, 1982
oil and charcoal on paper
30 x 34 (76.3 x 86.4)
Collection of Peter Carley, Washington, D.C.

9. *The Screen*, 1983
oil on canvas
88 x 113½ (223.5 x 285.8)
Collection of George and Betsy Frampton

10. *Untitled (Black Lingam)*, 1983–84
oil on canvas
26 x 30 (66.0 x 76.2)
Collection of Sandra and James F. Fitzpatrick

11. *Edge of Influence*, 1978–85
oil on canvas
22 x 22 (55.9 x 55.9)
Private Collection

12. *Untitled (Study for Kundalini Screen)*, 1985
gouache, watercolor, and pencil on paper
10¼ x 9½ (26.0 x 24.1)
Collection of the artist

13. *Untitled (Lotus)*, 1986
pencil and gesso on paper
25 x 21¾ (63.5 x 55.3)
Collection of Ann Willis

14. *The Garden*, 1985–87
oil on canvas
86 x 62½ (218.4 x 158.8)
Collection of Manfred Baumgartner

15. *Trees in the Backyard*, 1985–87
pencil, ink, and gouache on paper
9 x 12 (22.9 x 30.5)
Collection of the artist

16. *Saturn*, 1987
charcoal, pencil, and gouache on paper
22 x 29 (55.9 x 73.7)
Collection of Robin Rose and Judith Penski

17. *The Stones*, 1987
oil on canvas
28 x 22 (71.1 x 55.9)
Collection of Manfred Baumgartner

18. *Screen with Lotus*, 1978–88
pencil, charcoal, and oil pastel on paper
14 x 16½ (35.6 x 41.9)
Collection of the artist

19. *Untitled (Kalaśa)*, 1986–88
oil on canvas
86 x 109¼ (218.4 x 277.5)
Courtesy of Baumgartner Galleries, Washington, D.C., and Rosa Esman Gallery, New York

20. *Tea Vessel*, 1988
oil on canvas
18 x 20 (45.7 x 50.8)
Private Collection

21. *Heroes*, 1988
oil on canvas
38 x 48 (46.5 x 121.9)
Courtesy of Baumgartner Galleries, Washington, D.C., and Rosa Esman Gallery, New York

22. *Untitled (Blue Screen)*, 1988
oil on gessoed paper
31 x 45¾ (78.7 x 116.2)
Collection of John Macleod and Ann Klee

23. *Tree*, 1988
mixed media on paper
7¼ x 3¼ (18.4 x 8.3)
Collection of the artist

24. *Untitled (Black Moon)*, 1988
pencil, gouache, and watercolor on paper
13¾ x 10⅝ (34.9 x 27.0)
Courtesy of Baumgartner Galleries, Washington, D.C., and Rosa Esman Gallery, New York

25. *Untitled (Ledger)*, 1988
oil on canvas
68½ x 88½ (174.0 x 224.8)
Courtesy of Baumgartner Galleries, Washington, D.C., and Rosa Esman Gallery, New York

26. *Lotus Pond I*, 1989
pencil, pastel, oil crayon, and watercolor on paper
18 x 24 (45.7 x 61.0)
Courtesy of Baumgartner Galleries, Washington, D.C., and Rosa Esman Gallery, New York

27. *Untitled (Flyby)*, 1988–89
oil on canvas
16 x 20 (40.6 x 50.8)
Collection of the artist

28. *Haṁ Sa (The Gander)*, 1989
oil on canvas
75 x 88 (190.5 x 223.5)
Courtesy of Baumgartner Galleries, Washington, D.C., and Rosa Esman Gallery, New York

Acknowledgments

I would like to express my gratitude for the constant support and advice that Willem de Looper, Eliza Rathbone, and Laughlin Phillips have given to make this exhibition possible. On the Phillips Collection staff, I would like to thank Pat Nicholls and Becky Dodson for their help with the many details that went into organizing this exhibition. The realization of this publication would not have been possible without the creative design skills of Susan Lehmann and the sensitive editorial contributions of Ellen Cochran Hirzy. I wish to thank Manfred Baumgartner for his generous assistance with all aspects of the exhibition. Most of all, I would like to express my gratitude to Bill Willis for illuminating conversations, commitment, and tireless assistance in his collaboration on this exhibition.

Linda L. Johnson
Assistant Curator

William Willis would like to dedicate this exhibition to Gurumayi Chidvilasananda.